# 초등 영단어 750 따라쓰기

기획 : 와이앤엠 어학연구소

와이 앤 엠

# 차 례


1. 나, 너, 그… ⋯⋯⋯⋯⋯⋯⋯⋯⋯⋯⋯⋯⋯⋯⋯⋯⋯⋯⋯ 4
2. 우리 몸 · 숫자 · 액세서리 ⋯⋯⋯⋯⋯⋯⋯⋯⋯⋯ 10
3. 집과 가구 ⋯⋯⋯⋯⋯⋯⋯⋯⋯⋯⋯⋯⋯⋯⋯⋯⋯⋯⋯ 18
4. 가족 · 스포츠와 취미 ⋯⋯⋯⋯⋯⋯⋯⋯⋯⋯⋯⋯ 24
5. 음식과 식사 · 과일과 채소 ⋯⋯⋯⋯⋯⋯⋯⋯⋯ 32
6. 직업 · 인간과 삶 ⋯⋯⋯⋯⋯⋯⋯⋯⋯⋯⋯⋯⋯⋯⋯ 38
7. 학생과 학용품 · 경제 ⋯⋯⋯⋯⋯⋯⋯⋯⋯⋯⋯⋯ 44
8. 색과 장난감 · 친구와 사람 ⋯⋯⋯⋯⋯⋯⋯⋯⋯ 51
9. 탈것들 · 도시와 시설물 ⋯⋯⋯⋯⋯⋯⋯⋯⋯⋯⋯ 56
10. 언어 ⋯⋯⋯⋯⋯⋯⋯⋯⋯⋯⋯⋯⋯⋯⋯⋯⋯⋯⋯⋯⋯ 63

11. 때와 계절 · 나이와 숫자, 시간 · 방향 ⋯⋯⋯ 72
12. 동물 ⋯⋯⋯⋯⋯⋯⋯⋯⋯⋯⋯⋯⋯⋯⋯⋯⋯⋯⋯⋯⋯ 81
13. 우주와 자연 ⋯⋯⋯⋯⋯⋯⋯⋯⋯⋯⋯⋯⋯⋯⋯⋯⋯ 86
14. 대립어 ⋯⋯⋯⋯⋯⋯⋯⋯⋯⋯⋯⋯⋯⋯⋯⋯⋯⋯⋯⋯ 94
15. 움직임을 나타내는 단어 ⋯⋯⋯⋯⋯⋯⋯⋯⋯ 114
16. 모양이나 상태를 나타내는 단어 ⋯⋯⋯⋯⋯ 132
17. 부사 ⋯⋯⋯⋯⋯⋯⋯⋯⋯⋯⋯⋯⋯⋯⋯⋯⋯⋯⋯⋯⋯ 141
18. 전치사 ⋯⋯⋯⋯⋯⋯⋯⋯⋯⋯⋯⋯⋯⋯⋯⋯⋯⋯⋯ 145
· 찾아보기 ⋯⋯⋯⋯⋯⋯⋯⋯⋯⋯⋯⋯⋯⋯⋯⋯⋯ 148

# 초등 영단어 750 따라쓰기

# 1. 나, 너, 그...

**I**
나는, 내가
[ai 아이]

I I I I I I I I

**my**
나의
[maí 마이]

my my my my my

**me**
나를
[mi 미-]

me me me me me me

**you**
너, 당신
[ju: 유-]

you you you you

- I'm peter. I'm 10years old.
- This is my digital camera.
- Look at me!
- You look so pretty.

나는 Peter예요. 10살이죠.

이것은 제 디지털카메라예요.

나를 보세요.

너는 굉장히 예쁘다(너는 참 예쁘구나).

4

| **your** | your   your   your   your |
| --- | --- |
| 너의, 너희들의 | |
| [juəʳ 유얼] | |

| **he** | he   he   he   he   he |
| --- | --- |
| 그는, 그가 |  |
| [hiː 히-] | |

| **his** | his   his   his   his   his |
| --- | --- |
| 그의, 그의 것 | |
| [híz 히이스] | |

| **him** | him   him   him   him   him |
| --- | --- |
| 그를, 그에게 | |
| [him 힘] | |

| **she** | she   she   she   she |
| --- | --- |
| 그녀는, 그녀가 |  |
| [ʃiː 쉬] | |

- What is your name?  너의 이름은 무엇이니?
- He pointed the girl with a doll.  그는 인형을 가지고 있는 그 소녀를 가르켰어요.
- It is his umbrella.  그것은 그의 우산이야.
- She loves him.  그녀는 그를 사랑해요.
- She is really beautiful.  그녀는 정말 아름다워요.

## her
그녀의

[hə:r 허얼]

her　her　her　her

## it
그것은

[it 잇]

it  it  it  it  it  it  it  it

## its
그것의

[its 잇즈]

its its its its its its its its

## they
그들은

[ðei 데이]

they　they　they

## their
그들의

[ðɛər 데얼]

their　their　their　their

| | |
|---|---|
| · Jane is doing her homework. | Jane은 숙제하고 있어요. |
| · It is your dog. | 그것은 당신의 강아지예요. |
| · The baby is sleeping in its bed. | 갓난 아기는 침대에서 자고 있어요. |
| · They are going to school. | 그들은 학교에 가고 있어요. |
| · Their captain is very good. | 그들의 주장은 굉장히 좋은 사람이야. |

# them
그들을

[ðem 뎀]

them   them   them

# we
우리, 저희가

[wiː 위-]

we   we   we   we   we

# our
우리의

[auər아우월]

our our our our our our

# ours
우리의 것

[auərz아워즈]

ours   ours   ours   ours

# us
우리들을

[ʌs 어쓰]

us us us us us us us us

| | |
|---|---|
| · I told **them** to wait. | 나는 그들에게 기다리라고 말했어요. |
| · **We** go to school at 8 o'clock. | 우리는 8시에 등교한다. |
| · That building is **our** school. | 저 건물이 우리 학교야. |
| · Which car is **ours**? | 어느 것이 우리 차냐? |
| · He told **us** to stay home. | 그는 우리에게 집에 있으라고 했다. |

## this
이것

[ðis 디쓰]

this this this this this this

## these
이것들

[ðíːz 디-즈]

these   these   these

## that
저것, 그것

[ðæt 댓]

that that that that

## the
그

[ðə/ði 더/디]

the the the the the the

## those
그것들

[ðouz 도즈]

those those those those

- How about this shirt?
- These apples are red.
- Look at that! That is big!
- The girl is my sister.
- Those shoes are expensive.

이 셔츠는 어때요?
이 사과들은 빨갛다.
저것좀 봐! 크다!
그 소녀는 내 여동생입니다.
그 구두는 비싸다.

8

**there**
거기에
[ðɛər 데얼]

there there there there

**hers**
그녀의 것
[həːrz 허어즈]

hers hers hers

**mine**
나의 것
[máin 마인]

mine mine mine mine

**yours**
너의 것
[juərz 유어즈]

yours yours yours yours

| | |
|---|---|
| · Look over there. | 저기 좀 봐. |
| · This comic book is hers. | 이 만화책은 그녀의 것이야. |
| · The pen is mine. | 그 펜은 내거야. |
| · Yours is beautiful. | 너의 것은 예쁘다. |

# 2. 우리 몸 · 옷과 액세서리

## arm
팔

[aːrm 아-ㄹ암]

arm　arm　arm　arm

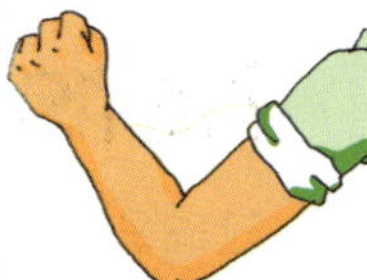

## back
등, 뒤

[bæk 백]

back　back　back　back

## body
몸, 신체

[bádi 바디]

body　body　body

## ear
귀

[iər 이얼]

ear　ear　ear　ear　ear　ear

---

- Tom's arm is long.
- I looked at his back.
- My whole body is aching now.
- Rabbits have long ears.

- Tom은 팔이 길어요.
- 난 그의 등을 보았어요.
- 지금 온몸이 아파요.
- 토끼의 귀는 길어요.

# eye
눈

[ai 아이]

eye　eye　eye　eye　eye

# face
얼굴

[feis 페이스]

face　face　face　face

# finger
손가락

[fíŋgər 휭거ㄹ]

finger　finger　finger

# foot
발

[fut 풋]

foot　foot　foot

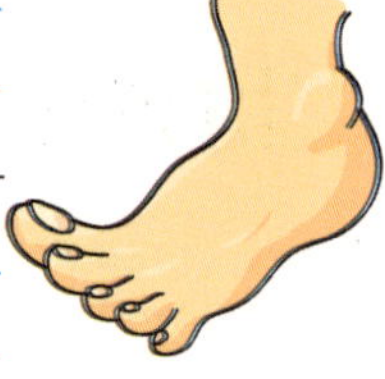

# hair
머리카락, 털

[hɛər 헤얼]

hair　hair　hair　hair　hair

| | |
|---|---|
| • Open your eyes and look around. | 눈을 뜨고 주위를 둘러보세요. |
| • I wash my face everyday. | 나는 매일 얼굴을 씻어요(세수해요). |
| • I touched water with my fingers. | 손가락으로 물을 만져보았어요. |
| • Peter is pushing the box with his foot. | Peter는 발로 상자를 밀고 있다. |
| • Her hair is black and short. | 그녀의 머리카락은 검고 짧아. |

## hand
손
[hænd 핸드]

hand    hand    hand    hand

## head
머리
[hed 헤드]

head    head    head

## heart
마음, 심장
[ha:rt하-ㄹ트]

heart    heart    heart    heart

## knee
무릎
[ni: 니-]

knee    knee    knee

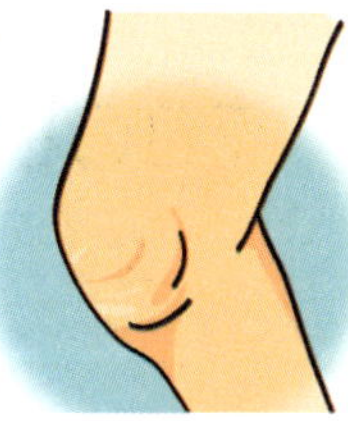

## leg
다리
[leg 렉]

leg    leg    leg    leg    leg

- We must wash our hands.
- His head touches the ceiling.
- The doctor is checking my heart.
- I feel pain in my knee.
- I broke my leg three days ago.

손을 꼭 씻어야 해요.
그의 머리는 천장에 닿아요.
의사 선생님이 제 심장을 검사하고 계세요.
무릎이 아파요.
3일전에 다리가 부러졌어요.

| **lip** 입술<br>[lip 립] | lip　lip　lip　lip　lip　lip |
| --- | --- |
| **mouth** 입<br>[mauθ 마웃쓰] | mouth　　mouth　 |
| **neck** 목<br>[nek 넥] | neck　neck　neck　neck |
| **nose** 코<br>[nouz 노우즈] | nose　nose　nose　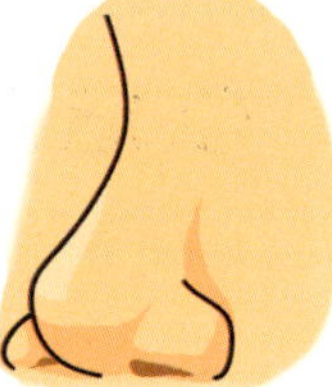 |
| **tooth** 이, 치아<br>[tuːθ 투-쓰] | tooth　tooth　tooth　tooth |

- Her lips turned purple with cold. 　추워서 그의 입술이 자줏빛이 되었다.
- Tom opened his mouth. 　Tom은 입을 벌렸어요.
- A neck is a part of our body. 　목은 우리 몸의 한 부분이다.
- We have a nose. 　우리는 하나의 코를 가지고 있다.
- Brush your tooth before you go to bed. 　자기전 이를 닦아라.

| **button**<br>단추, 버튼<br>[bʌ́tn 버튼] | button    button    button |
| **cap**<br>모자<br>[kæp 캡] | cap   cap   cap   cap  |
| **clothes**<br>옷<br>[klouðz클로우즈] | clothes   clothes   clothes |
| **coat**<br>외투<br>[kout 코옷] | coat  coat  coat  coat  coat |
| **dress**<br>의복<br>[dres 드뢰스] | dress   dress   dress  |

- The baby is touching the buttons.   아기가 단추를 만지고 있어요.
- Mom bought me this cap.   엄마가 이 모자를 사주셨어요.
- I'm making clothes for my cat.   지금 제 고양이에게 입힐 옷을 만들고 있어요.
- My grandfather bought me a blue coat.   할아버지께서 파란색 코트를 사주셨어요.
- I want to wear the pink dress.   분홍색 드레스(옷)를 입고 싶어요.

## glove
장갑

[glʌv 글러브]

glove glove glove glove

## hat
모자

[hæt 햇]

hat hat hat

## pants
바지

[pænts 팬츠]

pants pants pants

## pocket
호주머니

[pákit 파킷]

pocket pocket pocket

## ribbon
리본

[ríbən 뤼번]

ribbon ribbon

- I left my gloves at home.
- Mrs. Lee always wears a hat.
- Tom always wear same pants.
- She put her hand in her pockets.
- She wears red ribbon on her hair.

- 내 장갑을 집에 두고 왔어요.
- 이 선생님은 항상 모자를 쓰고 다니셔요.
- 탐은 항상 같은 바지를 입어.
- 그녀는 주머니에 손을 넣었어요.
- 그녀는 머리에 빨간 리본을 하고 있다.

**ring**
반지
[riŋ 륑]

ring   ring   ring

**shirt**
셔츠
[ʃə:rt 셔-ㄹ츠]

shirt   shirt   shirt   shirt

**shoe**
신, 구두
[ʃuː 슈-]

shoe   shoe   shoe   shoe

**skirt**
스커트
[skə:rt 스꺼얼트]

skirt   skirt   skirt

| | |
|---|---|
| • He gave me a ring. | 그가 나에게 반지를 주었어요. |
| • I bought this shirt last year. | 작년에 이 셔츠를 샀어요. |
| • My father bought a pair of shoes for me. | 아빠가 저에게 신발(한켤레)을 사주셨어요. |
| • That skirt looks cool. | 저 치마 멋져보여. |

## sock
양말

[sak 싹]

sock sock sock sock sock

## sweater
스웨터

[swétər스웨터]

sweater sweater sweater

## tie
넥타이

[tai 타이]

tie tie tie tie tie

## umbrella
우산

[ʌmbrélə엄브뤨러]

umbrella    umbrella

---

| | |
|---|---|
| · I'm looking for my red socks. | 나는 내 빨간 양말을 찾고 있다. |
| · This sweater is warm. | 이 스웨터는 따뜻하다. |
| · I must wear a tie tonight. | 저는 오늘 꼭 넥타이를 매야해요. |
| · He has an umbrella in his hand. | 그의 손에 우산이 있다(그는 우산을 들고 있어요). |

# 3. 집과 가구

**apartment**
아파트
[əpáːrtmənt 아파-알트먼트]

apartment　apartment

**basket**
바구니
[bǽskit 배스킷]

basket　basket　basket

**bed**
침대
[bed 뱃]

bed　bed　bed

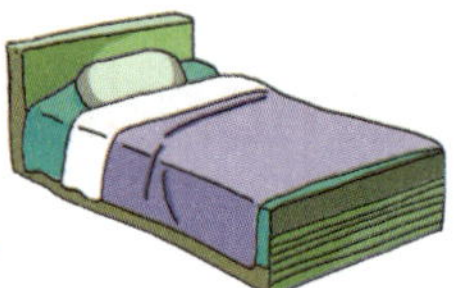

**bell**
종, 초인종
[bel 벨]

bell bell bell bell bell bell

- I really like my apartment.　나는 우리 아파트가 정말 좋아요.
- What do you have in your basket?　바구니 안에 뭐가 있어요?
- We have three beds.　우리는 침대가 3개 있어요.
- Listen! The bell is ringing.　들어봐~ 종이 울리고 있어.

## bench
긴 의자, 벤치
[bentʃ 벤취]

bench   bench   bench

## chair
의자
[tʃɛər 췌어ㄹ]

chair   chair   chair

## cup
컵
[kʌp 컵]

cup   cup   cup   cup   cup

## curtain
커튼
[kə́ːrtn 커튼]

curtain   curtain   curtain

## dish
접시
[diʃ 디쉬]

dish   dish   dish

- There are three benches in the park.    공원에는 벤치가 3개 있다.
- There is a cat under the chair.    의자 밑에 고양이 한 마리가 있어요.
- I bought this cup for mom.    나는 엄마 드리려고 이 컵을 샀어요.
- I hid behind the curtain.    전 커튼 뒤로 숨었어요.
- I sometimes help mom to wash the dishes.    저는 가끔 엄마가 설거지하는 것을 도와드려요.

## door
문

[dɔːr 도얼]

door　door　door　door

## fork
포크

[fɔːrk 포-ㄹ크]

fork　fork　fork

## garden
정원

[gáːrdn 가-ㄹ든]

garden　garden　garden

## gas
가스

[gæs 개스]

gas　gas　gas　gas

## glass
유리, 유리컵

[glæs 글래쓰]

glass　glass　glass　glass

---

- I knocked on the door.    나는 문을 두드렸어요.
- Give me a fork and knife.    제게 포크와 나이프를 주세요.
- There are roses in that garden.    저 정원엔 장미가 있어요.
- We filled the ballon with gas.    우리는 풍선에 가스를 채웠다.
- I drink three glasses of milk everyday.    나는 매일 우유를 세 잔씩 마셔요.

## home
집
[hóum 홈]

home home home

## house
집
[haus 하우스]

house house house

## key
열쇠
[kiː 키-]

key key key key key

## kitchen
부엌
[kítʃin 킷췬]

kitchen kitchen

## knife
칼
[naif 나이프]

knife knife knife knife

- I have to stay at home today.
- There is a big house on the hill.
- I lost my key yesterday.
- Refrigerator is in the kitchen.
- The knife is dangerous.

나는 오늘 집에 있어야만 해요.
언덕위에는 큰 집이 한 채 있어요.
저는 어제 열쇠를 잃어버렸어요.
냉장고는 부엌에 있어요.
그 칼은 위험해요.

## mirror
거울

[mírər 미뤄-ㄹ]

mirror mirror mirror

## radio
라디오

[réidióu 뢰이디오]

radio radio radio

## roof
지붕

[ruːf 루-프]

roof roof roof roof

## room
방

[ruːm 루-움]

room room room

## soap
비누

[soup 쏘웁]

soap soap soap soap

- She stands before a mirror all day.
- I often listen to the radio.
- Our house has a red roof.
- I usually study in my room.
- Wash your hand with soap.

그녀는 하루 종일 거울 앞에 서 있다.
나는 종종 라디오를 듣는다.
우리집에는 빨간 지붕이 있다.
나는 보통 내 방에서 공부해요.
비누로 손을 깨끗이 씻어라.

## sofa
소파
[sóufə 쏘우풔]

sofa sofa sofa

## spoon
숟가락, 스푼
[spuːn 스푸-ㄴ]

spoon spoon spoon

## stair
계단
[stɛər 스떼어]

stair stair stair stair

## telephone
전화
[téləfóun 텔레포운]

telephone telephone

## window
창(창문)
[wíndou 윈도우]

window window window

- The cushion is on the sofa.    그 쿠션은 소파 위에 있다.
- I ate my meal with a spoon.    나는 숟가락으로 식사를 했다.
- I went up stairs.    나는 계단을 올랐다.
- He is on the telephone.    그는 통화중이다.
- Please open the window.    창문 좀 열어 주세요.

# 4. 가족 · 스포츠와 취미

**birthday**
생일
[bə́ːrθdèi 벌쓰데이]

birthday   birthday

**brother**
형제
[brʌ́ðr 브롸덜]

brother   brother   brother

**cousin**
사촌, 친척
[kʌ́zn 커즌]

cousin   cousin   cousin

**dad/daddy**
아빠
[dæd 대드]

dad   dad   dad   dad   dad

---

- When is your birthday?    네 생일이 언제니?
- I have two younger brothers.    어린 남동생(형제)이 두 명 있어요.
- This is my cousin, Mike.    얘는 내 사촌 Mike야.
- Dad reads me some books at night.    아빠는 밤에 저에게 책을 읽어주셔요.

## daughter
딸

[dɔ́ːtər 더-러]

daughter    daughter

## family
가족

[fǽməli 페믈리]

family    family

## father
아버지

[fáːðər 퐈-덜]

father father father father

## grandmother
할머니

[grændmáːðər 그랜드머더]

grandmother

## ma'am
아주머니, 선생님(여교사)

[məm 맴]

ma'am    ma'am    ma'am

---

- My aunt has two daughters and a son.
- This is a picture of my family.
- I love my father.
- Grandmother likes to tell me interesting story.
- -Min-ho. -Yes, ma'am.

우리 이모는 1남 2녀(아들한명과 두 딸)를 두셨어요.

우리 가족 사진이예요.

전 아빠를 사랑해요.

할머니는 저에게 재밌는 얘기 해주시는 걸 좋아하셔요.

민호야. 예, 선생님.

## mom
엄마

[mam 맘]

mom　mom　mom　mom

## mother
어머니

[mʌ́ðər 머덜]

mother　mother

## parent
부모님

[péərənt 페어뤄ㄴ트]

parent　parent　parent

## sister
여자형제, 언니

[sístər 씨스털]

sister　sister　sister

## son
아들

[sɔn 썬]

son　son　son　son　son

- **Mom** got angry with me.    어머니가 나에게 화가 나셨다.
- She is my **mother**.    그녀는 나의 어머니예요.
- My **parents** are very nice.    나의 부모님은 매우 좋으신 분이예요.
- I have two **sisters**.    나는 두 명의 여자형제가 있어요.
- He is my **son**.    그는 나의 아들이다.

## uncle
아저씨, 삼촌

[ʌ́ŋkl 엉끌]

uncle uncle uncle

## art
미술, 예술

[ɑːrt 알트]

art  art  art  art  art  art

## ball
공

[bɔːl 버-얼]

ball  ball  ball  ball  ball  ball

## camera
카메라

[kǽmərə캐므러]

camera  camera

## club
클럽, 동호회

[klʌb 클럽]

club  club  club  club  club

| | |
|---|---|
| · I am going to my uncle's. | 나는 삼촌댁에 갈 거예요. |
| · My favorite subject is art. | 내가 가장 좋아하는 과목은 미술이다. |
| · This is my sister's ball. | 이건 우리 누나의 공이예요. |
| · I want to buy a new digital camera. | 새 디지털카메라를 사고 싶어요. |
| · He is my club friend. | 그는 내 동호회 친구야. |

| **exercise** 운동, 연습 [éksərsáiz 엑썰싸이즈] | exercise   exercise |
| **dance** 춤, 춤추다 [dæns 댄스] | dance dance dance  |
| **drum** 북, 드럼 [drʌm 드럼] | drum  drum  drum  drum |
| **film** 필름, 영화 [film 필름] | film  film  film  film  |
| **game** 게임 [geim 게임] | game  game  game |

- It's important to exercise everyday.    매일 운동하는 것은 중요해요.
- I like to dance.    저는 춤추는 걸 좋아해요.
- Peter is playing the drum.    Peter가 드럼을 치고 있어요.
- My parents like to go to see a film.    부모님은 영화보는 것을 좋아하세요.
- I like to play computer games.    컴퓨터 게임 하는 거 좋아해요.

**guitar**
기타
[gitá:r 기타-ㄹ]

guitar guitar guitar guitar

**movie**
영화
[mú:vi 무-뷔]

movie    movie    movie

**music**
음악
[mjú:zik 뮤-직]

music music music

**piano**
피아노
[piǽnou 애노우]

piano  piano  piano

**sing**
노래, 노래하다
[siŋ 씽]

sing  sing  sing  sing  sing

| | |
|---|---|
| · Can you play the guitar? | 기타 칠 줄 아세요? |
| · I went to the movie with my friends. | 나는 친구들과 영화를 보러 갔다. |
| · I like listening to music. | 나는 음악 듣는 것을 좋아한다. |
| · I can play the piano. | 나는 피아노 연주를 할 수 있어요. |
| · My hobby is to sing songs. | 내 취미는 노래 부르는 것이다. |

**skate**
스케이트
[skeit스케잇-트]

skate  skate  skate  skate

**soccer**
축구
[sákər싸커ㄹ]

soccer     soccer

**song**
노래
[sɔːŋ 쏭]

song  song  song  song

**sport**
스포츠
[spɔːrt스포-올트]

sport  sport  sport  sport

**swim**
수영하다, 수영
[swim 스윔]

swim  swim  swim

- Let's go skating!
- I played soccer with my friends.
- I sang a song for my parents.
- Soccer is a popular sport in korea.
- We went swimming last Sunday.

스케이트 타러가자!
나는 친구들과 축구를 했어요.
나는 부모님을 위해 노래를 불렀어요.
한국에서 축구는 인기가 좋다.
지난 일요일 우리는 수영하러 갔다.

**swing**
그네
[swiŋ 스윙]

swing  swing  swing

**team**
팀
[tiːm 팀]

team  team  team

**tennis**
테니스
[ténis 테니스]

tennis  tennis  tennis

**video**
비디오
[vídioú 브이디오]

video  video  video

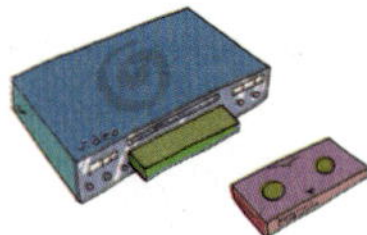

**violin**
바이올린
[váiəlín 봐이얼린]

violin  violin  violin

- There are two boys on the swing.   그네에 남자아이 둘이 타고 있다.
- His team won the game.   그의 팀이 게임에서 이겼다.
- She played tennis with her friend.   그녀는 친구와 함께 테니스를 쳤다.
- How often do you rent video tapes?   당신은 얼마나 자주 비디오 테이프를 빌려요?
- I can play the violin.   저는 바이올린을 연주할 수 있어요.

# 5. 음식과 식사 · 과일과 채소

**butter**
버터
[bʌ́tər 버러ㄹ]

butter butter butter butter

**breakfast**
아침식사
[brékfəst 브뢰ㄱ풔스트]

breakfast    breakfast

**bread**
빵
[bred 브레드]

bread  bread  bread

**cake**
케이크
[keik 케이크]

cake    cake    cake    cake

- There are bread and butter.    빵과 버터가 있어요.
- I ate bread and milk for breakfast.    나는 아침으로 빵과 우유를 먹었다.
- Tom, would like some bread?    Tom, 빵 좀 먹을래?
- She gave me a piece of cake.    그녀는 나에게 케이크 한 조각을 주었다.

## candy
사탕
[kǽndi 캔디]

candy candy candy

## cheese
치즈
[tʃiːz 취-즈]

cheese cheese cheese

## coffee
커피
[kɔ́ːfi 커-퓌]

coffee coffee coffee

## cream
크림
[kriːm 크뤼-임]

cream cream cream

## dinner
저녁 식사
[dínər 디널]

dinner dinner dinner

- Andy gave me a candy.
- Mice are eating cheese.
- Give me a cup of coffee.
- Put two spoons of cream.
- I had dinner with my friend, Tony.

- Andy가 나에게 사탕을 주었어요.
- 쥐들이 치즈를 먹고 있어요.
- 커피 한 잔 주세요.
- 크림 두 스푼을 넣으세요.
- 나는 친구 Tony와 저녁을 먹었어요.

# egg
달걀

[eg 엑]

egg egg egg egg

# food
음식

[fuːd 푸-드]

food food food food

# hamburger
햄버거

[hǽmbəːrgər 햄버거]

hamburger hamburger

# Juice
주스

[dʒúːs 쥬-스]

juice juice juice

# meat
고기

[miːt 미-잇트]

meat meat meat meat

- Chickens lay an egg each morning.
- What is your favorite food?
- Are you eating hamburger again?
- Would you like some juice?
- We will have meat for dinner.

- 닭은 매일 아침 달걀을 한 개씩 낳아요.
- 좋아하는 음식은 무엇인가요?
- 너 햄버거 또 먹는거야?
- 주스 좀 드실래요?
- 우리는 저녁식사로 고기를 먹을 거야.

## milk
우유
[milk 밀크]

milk  milk  milk  milk

## rice
쌀, 밥
[rais 롸이스]

rice  rice  rice  rice  rice

## salad
샐러드
[sǽləd 쌜러드]

salad  salad  salad

## salt
소금
[sɔːlt 써-얼트]

salt  salt  salt  salt  salt

## sugar
설탕
[ʃúgər 슈걸]

sugar  sugar  sugar  sugar

- **Milk** is good for our health.    우유는 건강에 좋다.
- Korean usually eat **rice**.    한국 사람들은 보통 밥을 먹는다.
- I ate some **salad** and chicken.    나는 샐러드와 치킨을 먹었다.
- Could you pass me the **salt**, please.    소금 좀 건내 주시겠어요?
- Do you like **sugar** in your coffee?    커피에 설탕 넣으시겠어요?

| **supper**<br>저녁식사<br>[sʌ́pər 써퍼얼] | supper    supper    supper |

| **apple**<br>사과<br>[ǽpəl 애쁠] | apple  apple  apple |

| **banana**<br>바나나<br>[bənǽnə 버내너] | banana    banana |

| **corn**<br>옥수수<br>[kɔːrn 콘] | corn corn corn corn corn |

| **cucumber**<br>오이<br>[kjúːkʌmbər 큐컴벌] | cucumber    cucumber |

- Supper is the last meal of the day.   저녁식사는 하루의 마지막 식사이다.
- Do you like apples?   사과 좋아하세요?
- I like bananas very much.   나는 바나나를 무척 좋아해요.
- Do you like corn?   옥수수 좋아하세요?
- A cucumber is long and green.   오이는 길고 녹색이다.

## fruit
과일

[fruːt 푸룻-트]

fruit　fruit　fruit　fruit　fruit

## grape
포도

[greip 그뢰입]

grape　grape　grape

## pear
(과일)배

[pɛər 페얼]

pear　pear　pear　pear

## strawberry
딸기

[strɔ́ːbéri 스트뤄-베뤼]

strawberry

## tomato
토마토

[təméitou 터메이토]

tomato　tomato　tomato

- What is your favorite fruit?
- Does Peter like grapes?
- This pear is sweet.
- I like strawberry.
- My mother likes tomato juice.

좋아하는 과일이 무엇인가요?
Peter는 포도를 좋아하나요?
이 배는 달다.
나는 딸기를 좋아해요.
엄마는 토마토주스를 좋아하세요.

# 6. 직업 · 인간과 삶

**captain**
선장, 우두머리
[kǽptin 캡틴]

captain　captain　captain

**cook**
요리사
[kúk 쿡]

cook　cook　cook

**doctor**
의사
[dάktər닥터ㄹ]

doctor　doctor　doctor

**job**
일, 직업
[dʒab 쫍]

job　job　job　job　job　job

- Mr. Han is the captain of the soccer team.　한선생님은 그 축구팀의 주장이에요.
- My mom is a great cook.　우리 엄마는 훌륭한 요리사다.
- I would like to be a doctor.　나는 의사가 되고 싶어요.
- "What's her job?"　그녀의 직업은 무엇인가요?

| **nurse**<br>간호사<br>[nə:rs 널쓰] | nurse  nurse  nurse |  |
| **pilot**<br>조종사<br>[páilət 파일럿] | pilot pilot pilot pilot pilot | |
| **police**<br>경찰<br>[pəlí:s펄리–스] | police  police  police |  |
| **course**<br>진로, 과정<br>[kɔ:rs코–ㄹ스] | course    course    course | |
| **god**<br>하느님<br>[gad 가드] | god    god    god    god | |

- She is a nurse.    그녀는 간호사이다.
- I want to be a pilot.    나는 조종사가 되고 싶어요.
- Police caught a thief.    경찰이 도둑을 잡았어요.
- The full course is finished now.    전 과정이 이제 끝났어요.
- Oh, God.    오, 신이시여.

| **group**<br>무리, 모임, 떼<br>[gruːp 구루웁] | group   group |  |
| **king**<br>왕<br>[kiŋ 킹] | king king king king |  |
| **lead**<br>인도하다<br>[iːd 리드] | lead lead lead lead lead | |
| **letter**<br>편지<br>[létər 레러-ㄹ] | letter letter letter letter | |
| **life**<br>생명, 생활<br>[laif 라이프] | life life life life life | |

- Each group has its flag.     각 그룹마다 깃발이 있어요.
- The lion is the king of animals.     사자는 동물의 왕이에요.
- Lead him to the place.     그를 그 장소로 인도하시오.
- I send a letter to my friend Min-su.     나는 친구 민수에게 편지를 보내요.
- Thank you for saving my life.     제 생명을 구해주셔서 감사해요.

| **live** | live live live live live |
|---|---|
| 살다 | |
| [liv 리브] | |

| **luck** | luck luck luck luck luck |
|---|---|
| 행운 | |
| [lɔk 럭] | |

| **mail** | mail mail mail |
|---|---|
| 우편 | |
| [meil 메일] | |

| **marry** | marry marry marry marry |
|---|---|
| 결혼하다 | |
| [mǽri 매뤼] | |

| **men** | men men men |
|---|---|
| man의 복수형 | |
| [men 멘] | |

- Where do you live?  사시는 곳이 어디예요?
- Good luck!  행운을 빌어요!
- I send a letter by mail.  나는 편지를 우편으로 보낸다.
- He will marry a woderful woman.  그는 멋진 여성과 결혼할 것이다.
- Most men like playing football.  대부분의 남자들은 축구하는 것을 좋아한다.

## news
소식
[njuːz 뉴-즈]

news　news　news

## party
파티, 모임
[páːrti파-ㄹ리]

party　party　party　party

## peace
평화
[piːs 피-스]

peace　peace　peace

## queen
여왕
[kwiːn퀴이-ㄴ]

queen queen queen

## sleep
잠자다
[sliːp슬리-입]

sleep　sleep　sleep　sleep

---

- Did you hear the news?　그 소식 들었어?
- Can you come to my party? 　내 파티에 올래?
- I want the world peace. 　나는 세계 평화를 원한다.
- A queen is the wife of a king. 　여왕은 왕의 아내이다.
- I went to sleep at 9 o'clock. 　나는 9시에 잤어요.

42

## stamp
우표, 인지

[stæmp 스탬프]

stamp    stamp

## town
마을

[táun 타운]

town  town  town  town

## village
마을, 촌락

[vílidʒ 빌리쥐]

village    village    village

## welcome
환영하다

[wélkəm 웰컴]

welcome welcome

---

- I like collecting stamps.　　　나는 우표 수집을 좋아해요.
- I live in town.　　　나는 마을에 살아요.
- The farmer lives in the village.　　　그 농부는 마을에 살아요.
- Welcome to Korea!　　　한국에 오신 걸 환영합니다!

# 7. 학생과 학용품 · 경제

**album**
앨범, 사진첩
[ǽlbəm 앨범]

album　album　album

**bag**
가방, 봉지
[bǽg 백]

bag　bag　bag　bag

**board**
판자, 게시판
[bɔːrd 보-르드]

board　board　board　board

**book**
책
[buk 북]

book　book　book　book

- Let's buy him a photo album.　그에게 사진첩(앨범)을 사주자.
- This is my schoolbag.　이건 제 책가방이예요.
- What's this new board for?　이 새 게시판은 어디에 쓸 거죠?
- Mom is reading a book for me.　엄마가 저에게 책을 읽어주고 계세요.

## camp
캠프
[kæmp 캠프]

camp   camp   camp   camp

## chalk
분필
[tʃɔːk 초어크]

chalk   chalk   chalk   chalk

## class
수업, 학급
[klæs 클래스]

class   class   class

## computer
컴퓨터
[kəmpjúːtər 컴퓨-러ㄹ]

computer   computer

## crayon
크레용
[kréiən 크래이언]

crayon   crayon   crayon

---

- Let's go camping.     캠핑하러 가자.
- Let's buy blackboard and chalk.     칠판과 분필을 삽시다.
- It's time to finish the class.     수업을 끝낼 시간이예요.
- There are three compurters on the desk.     책상위에 컴퓨터가 3대 있어요.
- I like to draw lines using crayons.     크래용으로 선긋는 것을 좋아해요.

## desk
책상

[desk 데스크]

desk   desk   desk   desk

## eraser
지우개

[iré isəʎéɤ 이뢰이줘르]

eraser eraser eraser

## ink
잉크

[iŋk 잉크]

ink   ink   ink   ink

## learn
배우다

[lə:ɾn 러-ㄹ언]

learn   learn   learn   learn

## lesson
수업

[lésn 렛쓴]

lesson   lesson   lesson

---

- There is a pencil on the desk.    책상 위에 연필 한 자루가 있어요.
- Tom, can I borrow your eraser?    Tom, 지우개 좀 빌려줄래?
- Uncle is filling the pen with ink.    삼촌이 펜에 잉크를 채워 넣고 계셔요.
- I want to learn English.    전 영어를 배우고 싶어요.
- I have no lesson today.    오늘은 수업이 하나도 없어요.

## library

도서관

[láibreri
라이브뢰뤼]

library  library  library

## page

페이지, 쪽

[peidʒ 페이쥐]

page  page  page  page

## paper

종이

[péipər 페이펄]

paper  paper  paper

## pen

펜

[pen 펜]

pen  pen  pen  pen

## pencil

연필

[pénsəl 펜쓸]

pencil  pencil  pencil

- Mom and I often go to a library.
- Open your page 6.
- I need a sheet of paper.
- Can I borrow your pen?
- Do you have pencils?

엄마랑 저는 가끔 도서관에 가요.
6쪽을 펴세요.
종이 한 장이 필요하다.
내가 네 펜을 빌릴 수 있을까? 혹은 펜좀 빌려줄래?
너 연필 있니?

## pin
핀
[pin 핀]

pin pin pin pin pin pin

## school
학교, 수업
[skuːl 스꾸-울]

school school school

## student
학생
[stjúːdənt 스츄-던트]

student student student

## study
공부하다
[stʌ́di 스떠디]

study study study study

## table
테이블
[téibl 테이블]

table table table

- Please, lend me a safety pin. 안전핀 좀 빌려 주시겠어요.
- After school, I came back home. 수업이 끝난 후, 나는 집으로 돌아 왔어요.
- How many students are there? 학생이 몇 명 있죠?
- At school, I study English. 학교에서, 나는 영어를 공부한다.
- There are two books on the table. 테이블 위에 책이 2권 있다.

## teach
**가르치다**

[tiːtʃ 티-취]

teach  teach  teach

## test
**시험, 검사**

[test 테스트]

test  test  test  test  test

## coin
**동전**

[kɔin 코인]

coin  coin  coin  coin  coin

## dollar
**달러ㄹ**

[dálər 달러ㄹ]

dollar  dollar  dollar  dollar

## market
**시장**

[máːrkit 마-ㄹ킷]

market  market

- She teaches English at our school.
- I had a test last Friday.
- Put the coins into that machine.
- It's ten dollars.
- I will buy apples at market.

그녀는 학교에서 영어를 가르친다.
지난 금요일에 나는 시험을 봤다.
저 기계에 동전을 집어넣으세요.
10달러입니다.
시장에서 사과를 살 거예요.

## money
돈
[mʌ́ni 머니]

money　money　money

## pay
지불하다
[pei 페이]

pay　pay　pay　pay　pay

## shop
가게
[ʃap 샵]

shop　shop　shop　shop

## store
가게, 상점
[stɔ́ːr 스또어-ㄹ]

store　store　store

## supermarket
슈퍼마켓
[súːpərmáːrkit 수-퍼ㄹ말킷]

supermatket　supermatket

---

- How much **money** do you have? 　 넌 돈이 얼마 있니?
- We **pay** the school expenses. 　 우리는 학비를 낸다.
- I went to the toy **shop**. 　 나는 장난감가게로 갔다.
- I came by a fruit **store**. 　 나는 과일 가게에 들렀다.
- I went to a **supermarket** to buy corn. 　 나는 옥수수를 사기 위해 슈퍼마켓에 갔다.

# 8. 색과 장난감 · 친구와 사람

**ballon**
풍선
[bəlú:n 벌루-운]

ballon ballon ballon

**black**
검은 색
[blæk 블랙]

black black black black

**blue**
파란색
[blu: 블루-]

blue blue blue

**brown**
갈색, 갈색의
[braun 브롸운]

brown brown brown

- Tom's balloon is very big.
- The prince has black hair.
- Jessica has blue eyes.
- My teacher wears brown jacket.

Tom의 풍선은 굉장히 커요.

왕자 머리카락은 검은색이에요.

Jessica의 눈은 파란색이예요.

선생님은 갈색 자켓을 입고 계시다.

## color
색깔
[kʌ́lər 컬러ㄹ]

color color color color

## doll
인형
[dal 덜]

doll doll doll doll

## gray
회색, 회색의
[grei 그뤠이]

gray gray gray gray

## orange
오렌지 색
[ɔ́ːrindʒ 오륀쥐]

orange orange

## pink
분홍
[piŋk 핑크]

pink pink pink pink

- What is your favorite color? — 가장 좋아하는 색이 뭐야?
- Susan and I are playing with a doll. — Susan과 나는 인형놀이를 하고 있어요.
- I like this gray sweater. — 나는 이 회색 스웨터가 좋아.
- Where is my orange shirt? — 내 오렌지색 셔츠 어디 있니?
- I like the pink. — 나는 분홍색을 좋아해요.

## red
빨간색, 붉은

[red 뤠드]

red red red red red red

## robot
로봇

[roubɔt 롸벗]

robot robot robot

## toy
장난감

[tɔi 터이]

toy toy toy toy toy

## white
흰, 흰빛

[hwait 와이트]

white white white white

## yellow
노랑

[jélou 옐로−]

yellow yellow

- She was red with shame.    그녀는 부끄러워서 얼굴이 빨개졌다.
- My dad gave me a robot.    아버지께서 로봇을 사 주셨어요.
- I played with toy.    나는 장난감을 가지고 놀았다.
- We can see the white color in the dark.    우리는 어둠 속에서 흰색을 볼 수 있다.
- The banana is yellow.    바나나는 노랑색이다.

## aunt
아주머니, 이모

[ænt 앤트]

aunt  aunt  aunt

## baby
아기

[béibi 베이비]

baby  baby  baby

## boy
소년

[bɔi 보이]

boy  boy  boy  boy  boy

## child
어린이

[tʃaild 촤일드]

child  child  child

## friend
친구

[frend 프뤠ㄴ드]

friend  friend  friend

---

- I love my aunt Amy. / 저는 Amy이모가 좋아요.
- The baby girl is my little sister. / 그 여자 아기는 내 여동생이예요.
- Who is that boy? / 저 소년은 누구니?
- The child always wishes to be a man. / 그 어린 아이는 항상 어른이 되기를 바래요.
- I have many friends. / 저는 친구가 많아요.

## girl

소녀

[gəːrl 거얼]

girl girl girl girl girl

## lady

숙녀, 부인

[léidi 레이디]

lady lady lady lady lady

## man

남자

[mæn 맨]

man man man man

## people

사람들, 국민

[píːpl 피-쁠]

people people people

---

| | |
|---|---|
| · That **girl** was wearing a blue skirt. | 그 소녀는 파란 치마를 입고 있었다. |
| · The **lady** over there is my aunt. | 저기 있는 숙녀분은 우리 고모에요. |
| · The **man** is my father. | 그 남자는 나의 아버지예요. |
| · **People** like flowers. | 사람들은 꽃을 좋아해요. |

# 9. 탈것들 · 도시와 시설물

**airplane**
비행기
[έərpléη 에얼플레인]

airplane  airplane  airplane

**ambulance**
구급차
[æmb앰뷸런스]

ambulance  ambulance

**bicycle**
자전거
[báisikəl바이시클]

bicycle  bicycle

**boat**
보트, 작은배
[bout 보웃트]

boat  boat  boat  boat

- I go to Busan by airplane.  나는 부산에 비행기로 간다.
- The ambulance is arriving.  구급차가 도착하고 있다.
- Can you ride a bicycle?  자전거를 탈 수 있나요?
- My uncle has a big boat.  삼촌은 큰 보트를 가지고 계신다.

## bus
버스

[bʌs 버스]

bus　bus　bus　bus　bus

## car
자동차

[kaːr 카-ㄹ]

car　car　car　car 

## ship
배

[ʃip 쉽]

ship　ship　ship　ship

## sled
썰매

[sled 슬레드]

sled　sled　sled　sled　sled

## subway
지하철

[sʌ́bwéi 써브웨이]

subway　subway 

- Look! Here comes a bus. | 봐봐! 버스가 온다.
- Let's get into this car. | 이 차를 탑시다.
- Look at that ship! | 저 배를 봐요!
- In winter, we sled. | 겨울에 우리는 썰매를 탄다.
- We went to In-cheon by subway. | 우리는 지하철로 인천에 갔다.

**taxi**
택시
[tǽksi 택씨]

taxi taxi taxi taxi

**train**
기차
[trein 츄뢰인]

train train train

**truck**
트럭
[trʌk 츄럭]

truck truck truck truck

**airport**
공항
[ɛərpɔ̀ːrt에어포-르트]

airport airport

**bank**
은행
[bæŋk 뱅크]

bank bank bank bank

- I took a taxi to the airport.  공항까지 택시를 타고 갔다.
- I will travel by train.  나는 기차로 여행할거예요.
- The truck is big.  저 트럭은 크다.
- Is there a bus to airport?  공항으로 가는 버스가 있어요?
- My father works for that bank.  우리 아빠는 저 은행에서 일하셔요.

## bridge
다리
[bridʒ브릿쥐]

bridge    bridge

## capital
수도, 서울
[kǽpitl캐피틀]

capital    capital    capital

## church
교회
[tʃəːtʃ춰-ㄹ취]

church    church

## city
도시
[síti 씨티]

city city city city city city

## floor
바닥, 층
[flɔːr플로-월]

floor    floor    floor    floor

---

- We walked across the bridge.
- Seoul is the capital of Korea.
- I go to church on Sundays.
- There are lots of people in the city.
- The book store is on the third floor.

우리는 걸어서 다리를 건넜어요.
서울은 대한민국의 수도예요.
저는 일요일마다 교회에 가요.
이 도시에는 사람들이 아주 많아요.
그 서점은 3층에 있어요.

## gate
문, 출입구
[geit 게잇트]

gate  gate  gate  gate

## hospital
병원
[háspitl 하스피틀]

hospital  hospital  hospital

## hotel
호텔
[houtél 호텔]

hotel  hotel  hotel  hotel

## office
사무실
[ɔ́:fis 어-퓌스]

office  office  office

## paint
페인트
[peint 페인트]

paint  paint  paint

- There is a dog at the gate.
- Ted is in the hospital.
- How about staying in a hotel?
- He works hard in his office.
- Pass me that can of paint, please.

문 앞에 개가 한 마리 있어요.
Ted는 병원에 입원해 있어요.
호텔에 묵는 건 어때요?
그는 그의 사무실에서 열심히 일한다.
그 페인트통 좀 건네줘요.

## picnic
소풍
[píknik 피크닉]

picnic picnic picnic

## place
장소, 곳
[pleis 플레이스]

place place place place

## restaurant
레스토랑
[réstərənt 뢰스토뤈트드]

restaurant restaurant

## road
길, 도로
[roud 로우드]

road road road

## seat
자리, 좌석
[siːt 씨-잇트]

seat seat seat seat

- We went on a picnic last weekend.
- The place is very nice.
- We had a dinner at restaurant.
- The road is narrow.
- Please, have a seat.

우리는 지난 주말에 소풍을 갔다.
그 장소는 매우 멋져.
우리는 레스토랑에서 저녁을 먹었어요.
그 도로는 좁아요.
앉으세요.

| **station**<br>역, 정거장<br>[stéiʃən 스때이션] | station　station |  |
| **street**<br>거리<br>[strit 스뜨뤼-ㅅ] | street  street  street  street | |
| **travel**<br>여행, 여행하다<br>[trǽvəl 튜뢰블] | travel  travel  travel  travel | |
| **trip**<br>여행<br>[trip 츄뤄ㅂ] | trip　trip　trip　trip |  |

- I wait for taxi at the station.　나는 정거장에서 택시를 기다린다.
- Let's cross the street.　길을 건너자.
- I want to travel around the world.　나는 전세계를 여행하고 싶어요.
- How was your trip?　이거 해보자!(이거 시도해보자)

# 10. 언 어

**and**
그리고, ~와
[ænd 앤드]

and　and　and　and　and

**ask**
묻다, 질문하다
[æsk 애스크]

ask　ask　ask　ask

**because**
왜냐하면
[bikɔ́:z비커-즈]

because　because

**but**
그러나, 하지만
[bʌt 벗]

but　but　but　but　but

- I like hamburger and pizza.　나는 햄버거와 피자를 좋아해.
- "What are you doing?" Mom asked.　"뭐하고 있니?" 엄마가 물어보셨어요.
- I like Tom because he is kind.　나는 Tom이 좋아요. 왜냐하면 친절하니까요.
- He likes apples. But I don't.　그는 사과를 좋아해요. 그러나 저는 안 좋아해요.

| **bye** <br> (헤어질 때)안녕 <br> [bai 바이] | bye　bye　bye |  |

| **dictionary** <br> 사전 <br> [díkʃəneri딕셔네뤼] | dictionary　　dictionary | |

| **example** <br> 보기, 예 <br> [igzǽmpl 이그젬쁠] | example　　example | |

| **hear** <br> 듣다 <br> [hiər 히얼] | hear hear hear hear hear | |

| **hello** <br> 안녕, 여보세요 <br> [helóu 헬로우] | hello　hello　hello |  |

- "Good bye~ see you later." — "안녕~ 다음에 보자"
- Can I borrow your dictionary? — 당신의 사전을 빌릴 수 있을까요?
- Can you give me an example? — 예를 하나 들어볼래?
- Can you hear me? — 내말 들리니?
- "Hello, may I speak to Tom?" — 여보세요, tom이랑 통화할 수 있을까요?

## how
어떻게, 얼마나
[hau 하우]

how　how　how　how

## idea
생각
[aidíːə 아이디어]

idea　idea　idea　idea

## listen
듣다
[lísn 리쓴]

listen　listen　listen　listen

## matter
문제, 곤란
[mǽtər 매터]

matter　matter　matter

## question
질문
[kwéstʃən 퀘스쳔]

question　question

---

- **How** are you?　어떻게 지내니?
- Do you have any **ideas**?　무슨 좋은 생각 있어?
- I **listen** to the music everyday.　나는 매일 음악을 듣는다.
- What is the **matter** with you?　무슨 일이야?
- Please answer my **question**.　질문에 대답해 주세요.

## quiz
질문, 퀴즈
[kwíz 퀴즈]

quiz　quiz　quiz

## read
읽다, 낭독하다
[riːd 뤼-드]

read read read read

## say
말하다
[sei 세이]

say　say　say　say　say

## speak
말하다
[spiːk 스삑-ㅋ]

speak　speak　speak

## spell
철자
[spel 스뻴]

spell　spell　spell　spell

- I'll give you a quiz. 　내가 퀴즈 하나 낼께요.
- I read a book loudly. 　나는 책을 큰소리로 읽었다.
- Don't say no. 　안 된다고 말하지 마세요.
- I can speak English. 　나는 영어를 말할 수 있어요.
- How do you spell this word? 　이 단어의 철자가 어떻게 되나요?

## story
이야기
[stɔ́ːri 스토뤼]

story　story　story　story

## talk
말하다
[tɔːk 터-억]

talk　talk　talk

## tell
말하다
[tel 텔]

tell　tell　tell　tell　tell

## think
~라고 생각하다
[θiŋk 씽크]

think　think　think　think

## what
무엇, 어떤
[hwat 왓]

what　what　what

- Mom likes to tell me some stories. / 엄마는 나에게 얘기해 주시는 걸 좋아하신다.
- What are you talking about? / 너네 무슨 얘기하는 중이야?
- Don't tell a lie. / 거짓말을 하지 마라.
- I think it is wrong. / 나는 그것이 틀렸다고 생각한다.
- What are you doing? / 뭐하고 있니?

**when**
언제
[*h*wen 웬]

when　when　when　when

**where**
어디에
[*h*wɛər 웨얼]

where　　where

**which**
어느쪽, 어느
[*h*witʃ 윗취]

which　　which　　which

**who**
누구
[*h*uː 후–]

who　　who　　who

**whom**
누구를
[*h*uːm 후우–ㅁ]

whom　　whom　　whom

- **When** is your birthday?　생일이 언제야?
- **Where** are you from?　어디 출신이야?
- **Which** one is better?　어떤게 더 좋아?
- **Who** is he?　그는 누구야?
- **Whom** did you meet yesterday?　어제 누구를 만났어?

68

**whose**
누구의
[*hu:z* 후-즈]

whose   whose

**why**
왜
[*h*wai 와이]

why  why  why  why  why

**word**
낱말, 단어
[wəːrd 워드]

word  word  word  word

**yes**
예, 네
[jes 예스]

yes  yes  yes  yes

**am**
~이다
[æm 엠]

am  am  am  am  am

| | |
|---|---|
| · **Whose** daughter is she? | 누구의 딸이야? |
| · **Why** do you cry? | 왜 우니? |
| · How do you spell this **word**? | 이 단어 철자가 어떻게 되죠? |
| · **Yes**, ma'am. | 네, 선생님 |
| · I **am** a student. | 나는 학생이다. |

| **are** <br> ~이다 <br> [aːr 아-르] | are   are   are   are   are |
| **be** <br> ~이다 <br> [biː 비-] | be   be   be   be   be  |
| **did** <br> 했다, 했었다 <br> [did 디드] | did   did   did   did   did |
| **do** <br> 하다 <br> [duː 드] | do   do   do   do   do  |

| | |
|---|---|
| · We **are** good friends. | 우리들은 사이좋은 친구예요. |
| · He must **be** hungry. | 그는 배고픈 게 틀림 없어. |
| · I **did** a lot of things yesterday. | 어제 많은 일들을 했어요. |
| · What did you **do** last weekend? | 지난 주에 뭐했니? |

## does
do의 3인칭 단수

[dʌz 더즈]

does　does　does　does

## is
~에 있다

[íz 이즈]

is　is　is　is　is　is

## was
am, is의 과거형

[wʌz 워즈]

was　was　was　was　was

## were
are의 과거형

[wə:r 워-ㄹ]

were　were　were　were

| | |
|---|---|
| • What **does** she play? | 그녀는 무엇을 연주했니? |
| • There **is** a cup of coffee on the table. | 식탁 위에 커피 한 잔이 있어요. |
| • He **was** a student. | 그는 학생이었다. |
| • We **were** students. | 우리는 학생이었다. |

**afternoon**
오후
[ǽftərnúːn 애프터ㄹ누-운]

afternoon afternoon

**April**
4월
[éiprəl에이쁘럴]

April    April    April    April

**autumn**
가을
[ɔ́ːtəm 어-틈]

autumn    autumn

**calendar**
달력
[kǽləndər캘린더얼]

calendar    calendar

- I met him in the afternoon.  나는 그를 오후에 만났어요.
- I was born in April.  나는 4월에 태어났어요.
- It is windy in the autumn.  가을에는 바람이 많이 불어요.
- There is a calendar on the wall.  벽에 달력이 있어요.

## date
날짜

[deit 데잇트]

date　date　date

## day
낮, 하루

[dei 데이]

day day day day day day

## evening
저녁

[íːvniŋ 이-브닝]

evening　evening

## fall
가을

[fɔːl 풔ㄹ]

fall fall fall fall fall fall

## holiday
휴일, 공휴일

[hálədéi 할러데이]

holiday　holiday　holiday

- What's the date today?    오늘 몇일이에요?(오늘 날짜가 어떻게 되죠?)
- I play all day long every day.    난 매일 하루 종일 놀아요.
- I feel tired in the evening.    나는 저녁에는 피곤해.
- In fall, we can see many leaves.    가을에는 낙엽을 많이 볼 수 있어요.
- Did you have a good holiday?    휴일 잘 보내셨어요?

| **lunch** | lunch  lunch  lunch  lunch |
| :-- | :-- |
| 점심 |  |
| [lʌntʃ 런취] |  |

| **morning** | morning     morning |
| :-- | :-- |
| 아침 |  |
| [mɔ́ːrniŋ 모–ㄹ닝] |  |

| **night** | night  night  night |
| :-- | :-- |
| 밤 |  |
| [nait 나잇] |  |

| **noon** | noon  noon  noon  noon |
| :-- | :-- |
| 정오, 한 낮 |  |
| [nuːn 눈] |  |

| **season** | season   season   season |
| :-- | :-- |
| 계절 |  |
| [síːzn 씨–즌] |  |

- It's time for lunch. / 점심 먹을 시간이에요.
- Good morning! / 좋은 아침!
- I stayed up all night. / 나는 밤새도록 깨어 있었다.
- We have lunch at noon. / 우리는 정오에 점심을 먹는다.
- What's your favorite season? / 가장 좋아하는 계절은?

## spring
봄
[spriŋ 스프링]

spring  spring

## summer
여름
[sʌ́mər 써머ㄹ]

summer  summer

## today
오늘
[tudéi 투데이]

today  today  today

## tomorrow
내일
[təmɔ́ːrou 투머-로우]

tomorrow  tomorrow

## tonight
오늘 밤
[tənáit 터나잇]

tonight  tonight  tonight

---

- I like spring.  난 봄이 좋아요.
- In summer, it is hot.  여름에는 더워요.
- Today is my birthday.  오늘은 내 생일이다.
- Tomorrow will be cold.  내일은 추울 거야.
- Tonight will be snowy.  오늘밤엔 눈이 올 거야.

**week**
주, 1주간
[wiːk 위-크]

week  week  week  week

**winter**
겨울
[wíntər원터얼]

winter  winter  winter

**yesterday**
어제
[jéstərdéi 예스털데이]

yesterday  yesterday

**a**
하나의, 한사람의
[ə 어]

a  a  a  a  a  a  a  a

**age**
나이
[eidʒ 에이쥐]

age  age  age  age  age

- I will travel America for a week. / 나는 일주일동안 미국을 여행할 거야.
- It's cold in winter. / 겨울엔 추워요.
- Yesterday was my brother's birthday. / 어제는 내 남동생의 생일이었다.
- There is a book on the desk. / 책상 위에 책이 한 권 있다.
- At the age of 10, I went to Italy. / 열살 때 저는 이탈리아로 갔어요.

| **an**<br>하나의<br>[æn 언] | an　an　an　an　an　an |
| **four**<br>4, 4의<br>[fɔːr 포-] | four　four　four　four　four |
| **half**<br>반, 2분의1<br>[hæf 해프] | half　half　half　half　half |
| **hour**<br>시간<br>[auər 아우월] | hour　hour　hour  |
| **hundred**<br>백(100)<br>[hʌndrəd 헌드뤗] | hundred　　hundred |

- There is **an** album on the desk.　책상에 앨범이 한 권 있다.
- My family is **four**.　우리 가족은 4명입니다.
- Please cut this bread in **half**.　이 빵을 반으로 잘라주세요.
- Peter slept for five **hours**.　Peter는 5시간동안 잤어요.
- My grandfather is one **hundred** years old.　할아버지는 100세이십니다.

| **minute**<br>분<br>[mínit 미닛] | minute   minute   minute |
| **million**<br>100만<br>[míljən밀리언] | million   million   million |
| **number**<br>수, 숫자<br>[nʌ́mbəɾ넘벌] | number   number |
| **o'clock**<br>~시(정각)<br>[əklák 어클락] | o'clock   o'clock |
| **set**<br>한 벌, 짝, 세트<br>[set 세엣] | set  set  set  set  set |

- We have only 5 **minutes**.     우리는 오직 5분의 시간이 없어(우리는 5분밖에 시간이 없어).
- He has one **million** won.     그는 백만 원이 있어요.
- The **number** is two.     그 숫자는 2이다.
- It is 6 **o'clock**.     6시예요.
- I have a **set** of gloves.     나는 장갑 한 쌍이 있다.

## time
시각, 시간
[taim 타임]

time   time   time   time

## year
년, 나이
[jiər 이열]

year   year   year

## zero
0, 영
[zíərou 지로우]

zero   zero   zero   zero

## east
동쪽
[iːst 이스트]

east   east   east

## map
지도
[mæp 맵]

map   map   map   map

- What **time** is it?     지금 몇 시죠?
- Happy new **year**!     새해 복 많이 받으세요!
- '0' is called **zero**.     0은 영이라고 부른다.
- Go **east**.     동쪽으로 가.
- I marked my house on the **map**.     우리(나의)집을 지도에 표시했다.

| **north** 북쪽<br>[nɔːrθ노-ㄹ쓰] | north  north  north  north |
| **south** 남쪽<br>[sauθ싸웃쓰] | south  south  south  |
| **visit** 방문하다<br>[vízit 뷔짓] | visit  visit  visit  visit |
| **way** 길, 방법<br>[w ei 웨이] | way  way  way  way  |
| **west** 서쪽<br>[w est 웨스트] | west  west  west  west |

- My house stands in the north of Seoul. — 우리 집은 서울의 북쪽에 있다.
- The man went south. — 그는 남쪽으로 갔다.
- Can you visit me, today? — 오늘 절 방문해 줄 수 있나요?
- There is no way through. — 통로가 없어요.
- The sun sets in the west. — 해는 서쪽으로 진다.

# 12. 동 물

**animal**
동물, 짐승
[ǽnəməl 애니멀]

animal　animal　animal

**ant**
개미
[ænt 앤트]

ant　ant　ant　ant

**bear**[1]
곰
[bɛər 베어-ㄹ]

bear　bear　bear

**bird**
새
[bə:rd 버얼드]

bird　bird　bird　bird

- A bear is a big **animal**.　곰은 몸집이 큰 동물이에요.
- The **ants** are diligent.　개미들은 부지런하다.
- **Bears** like honey.　곰은 꿀을 좋아해.
- **Birds** fly in the air.　새들은 공중을 날아다녀요.

| **cat**<br>고양이<br>[kæt 캣] | cat   cat   cat   cat |  |

**chicken** 닭 [tʃíkən 취킨]

chicken  chicken  chicken

**cow** 암소, 젖소 [kau 카우]

cow  cow  cow  cow  cow

**deer** 사슴 [diər 디얼]

deer  deer  deer

**dog** 개 [dɔːg 더―ㄱ]

dog  dog  dog  dog  dog

- I'm afraid of cats.    저는 고양이가 무서워요.
- The chickens make a lot of noise.    닭들이 너무나 시끄럽게 해요.
- Cows make milk."    암소들은 우유를 만들어요.
- Have you ever seen a deer?    사슴을 본 적이 있니?
- How many dogs are in the playground?    운동장에 개가 몇 마리나 있나요?

## duck
오리
[dʌk 덕]

duck   duck   duck   duck

## elephant
코끼리
[éləfənt 엘러풔ㄴ트]

elephant     elephant

## fish
물고기
[fiʃ 퓌쉬]

fish   fish   fish   fish

## fly(2)
파리
[flai 플롸이]

fly   fly   fly   fly   fly   fly

## fox
여우
[faks ]

fox  fox  fox  fox  fox  fox

- The ducks can't fly.    오리는 날 수 없다.
- The elephants are very strong.    코끼리는 매우 힘이 세다.
- Did you catch any fish?    고기 좀 잡으셨어요?
- Frog eats fly.    개구리는 파리를 먹어요.
- A fox is a wild animal.    여우는 야생 동물이다.

# hen
암탉

[hen 헨]

hen hen hen hen

# horse
말

[hɔːrs 호올스]

horse horse horse

# lion
사자

[láiən 라이언]

lion lion lion lion lion

# mice
mouse의 복수형

[mɑís 마이스]

mice mice mice mice

# monkey
원숭이

[mʌ́ŋki 멍끼]

monkey monkey

- **Hen** lays an egg.
- Riding a **horse** is very funny.
- A **lion** found a zebra.
- **Mice** like chees.
- **Monkeys** like bananas.

암탉은 계란을 낳아요.
말타는 건 재밌어요.
사자가 얼룩말을 발견했어요.
쥐들은 치즈를 좋아한다.
원숭이들은 바나나를 좋아해요.

## pig
돼지
[pig 픽]

pig pig pig pig pig

## sheep
양
[ʃiːp 쉽]

sheep sheep sheep sheep

## tiger
호랑이
[táigər 타이걸]

tiger tiger tiger

## zoo
동물원
[zuː 주—]

zoo zoo zoo zoo zoo zoo

- Pigs eat a lot.
- I have never seen sheep.
- Have you ever seen a tiger?
- Let's go to the zoo.

돼지는 많이 먹어요.
나는 양을 본 적이 없어요.
너는 호랑이를 본 적 있니?
동물원에 가자.

# 13. 우주와 자연

**air**
공기
[ɛər 에어ㄹ]

air air air air air

**beach**
물가, 바닷가
[biːtʃ 비-잇취]

beach beach beach beach

**cloud**
구름
[klaud 클라우드]

cloud cloud cloud

**country**
나라, 지역
[kʌ́ntri 컨츠뤼]

country country country

- We would die without air.     우리는 공기가 없으면 죽고 말 거야.
- We will go to beach.     나는 올 여름 바닷가에 가고 싶어요.
- The birds fly over the clouds.     새들이 구름 위로 날아다녀요.
- My grandmother lives in the country.     할머니는 시골에서 사셔요.

## earth
지구, 땅

[ə:r𝜃어-르쓰]

earth earth earth earth

## field
들판

[fi:ld퓌-르드]

field field field field

## grass
풀

[græs 그뢰쓰]

grass grass grass grass

## gold
금

[gould 고울드]

gold gold gold gold

## green
녹색

[gri:n 그뤼인]

green green green green

- There are a lot of animals on the earth.
- The farmer works in the field.
- "Keep off the grass."
- This box is full of gold.
- I like green color.

지구에는 많은 동물들이 있어요.
농부가 들판에서 일을 해요.
잔디에 들어가지 마시오.
이 상자는 금으로 가득 차 있어요.
저는 녹색을 좋아해요.

## ground
땅, 운동장
[graund 그라운드]

ground    ground

## hill
언덕
[hil 힐]

hill hill hill hill hill hill

## ice
얼음
[ais 아이스]

ice ice ice ice ice ice

## island
섬
[áilənd아일런드]

island island island

## jungle
밀림, 정글
[dʒʌ́ŋgl쥐어글]

jungle jungle jungle jungle

---

- Let's play at the ground.     운동장에서 놀자.
- A cottage is on a hill.     언덕 위에 작은집이 하나 있다.
- I slipped on the ice.     나는 얼음판에서 넘어졌어요.
- I have never been to the island.     나는 그 섬에 가본 적이 없어요.
- The lion is king of the jungle.     사자는 밀림의 왕이에요.

## light(2)
빛, 조명
[lait 라잇트]

light　light　light　light

## lake
호수
[leik 레익]

lake lake lake lake

## land
땅, 육지
[lænd 랜드]

land land land land

## leaf
나뭇잎
[li:f 리-프]

leaf leaf leaf leaf leaf leaf

## month
달
[mʌnθ 먼쓰]

month　month　month

- Don't forget to turn off the light.
- There are many lakes in Canada.
- I traveld over land and sea last year.
- Look! The red leaf is falling.
- I go to movies once a month.

불(조명) 끄는 것 잊지 마!
캐나다에는 호수가 많아요.
나는 작년에 육지와 바다를 여행했다.
봐봐! 빨간 나뭇잎이 떨어지고 있어.
나는 한 달에 한 번 영화를 보러 가요.

| **moon**<br>달<br>[muːn 무-ㄴ] | moon moon moon |  |
| **mountain**<br>산<br>[mauntən 마운튼] | mountain mountain | |
| **plant**<br>식물<br>[plænt 플랜트] | plant plant plant plant | |
| **pool**<br>웅덩이, 연못<br>[puːl 푸-울] | pool pool pool pool pool | |
| **rain**<br>비, 비가오다<br>[rein 뢰인] | rain rain rain rain |  |

- There is a moon.
- I climbed a mountain last Saturday.
- The plants need water.
- Fish are in the pool.
- I walked in the rain.

달이 떴다.
나는 지난 토요일 산에 올랐어요.
식물은 물이 필요하다.
연못에 물고기들이 있어요.
나는 빗속을 걸었어요.

| **rainbow**<br>무지개<br>[réinbóu 뢰인보우] | rainbow  rainbow  rainbow |
| **river**<br>강<br>[rívər 뤼버-ㄹ] | river    river    river  |
| **sand**<br>모래<br>[sænd 쌘드] | sand  sand  sand  sand |
| **sea**<br>바다<br>[siː 씨-] | sea  sea  sea  sea  |
| **silver**<br>은, 은빛, 은의<br>[sílvər 씰뷔얼] | silver  silver  silver  silver |

- we can see a rainbow after it rains. — 비가 오고 난 후에는 무지개를 볼 수 있다.
- I jumped into the river. — 나는 강에 뛰어 들었어요.
- We built sand castles. — 우리는 모래성을 쌓았다.
- I went to the sea last summer. — 나는 지난 여름에 바다에 갔어요.
- He gave me a silver ring. — 그는 나에게 은반지를 주었다.

## sky
하늘

[skai 스까이]

sky   sky   sky   sky   sky   sky

## snow
눈, 눈이오다

[snou 스노우]

snow   snow   snow

## space
공간, 우주

[speis 스뻬이스]

space   space   space   space

## star
별

[staːr 스따-ㄹ]

star   star   star   star

## sun
태양, 햇빛

[sʌn 썬]

sun   sun   sun   sun   sun

---

- Look at the blue sky!     저 파란 하늘을 봐!
- It is snowing.     눈이 오고 있다.
- The people are looking for a parking space.     사람들이 주차할 공간을 찾고 있다.
- It is hard to see stars in the city.     도시에서는 별을 보기 힘들다.
- The sun rises in the east.     해는 동쪽에서 뜬다.

| | |
|---|---|
| **tree** 나무 [tri: 츄뤼-] | tree   tree   tree   tree   tree |
| **water** 물 [wɔ́:tər 워-터] | water   water   water  |
| **wind** 바람 [wind 윈드] | wind   wind   wind  |
| **wood** 나무, 숲 [wud 우드] | wood   wood   wood   wood |
| **world** 세계, 지구 [wə:rld 워-ㄹ드] | world   world   world   world |

- The tree is older than I. — 저 나무는 나보다 나이가 많아요.
- People drink water every day. — 사람들은 물을 매일 마신다.
- The paper is swing in the wind. — 그 종이가 바람에 흔들린다.
- I walked in the wood. — 나는 숲속을 걸었어요.
- I want to travel all over the world. — 나는 전 세계를 여행하고 싶다.

# 14. 대립어

**large**
큰
[laːrdʒ 라-ㄹ쥐]

large　large　large　large

**thin**
얇은
[θin 띤]

thin　thin　thin　thin

**fat**
뚱뚱한
[fæt 퓌앳]

fat　fat　fat　fat　fat　fat

**heavy**
무거운
[hévi 헤뷔]

heavy　heavy　heavy

- I want large size skirt.　전 큰 사이즈 치마를 원해요.
- This book is very thin.　이 책은 정말 얇아요.
- My cat is little fat, but very cute.　우리 고양이는 조금 뚱뚱하지만 귀여워요.
- Elephants are really heavy.　코끼리는 아주 무겁다.

94

## small
작은

[smɔːl 스모-ㄹ]

small  small  small  small

## thick
두꺼운

[θik 씩]

thick  thick  thick

## thin
얇은

[θin 띤]

thin  thin  thin  thin  thin

## light(1)
가벼운

[lait 라잇트]

light  light  light

- The ball is small. — 그 공은 작다.
- How thick is it? — 그건 두께가 얼마나 되죠?
- She is very thin. — 그녀는 매우 날씬해요.
- Tom is lighter than his brother. — Tom은 그의 형보다 가벼워요.

## quick
빠른
[kwik 퀵]

quick quick quick

## sell
팔다
[sel 쎌]

sell sell sell sell sell sell

## much
많은
[mʌtʃ 멋취]

much much much much

## many
많은
[méni 매니]

many many many

## little
작은
[lítl 리를]

little little little little

- He is quick to learn.    그는 배우는 속도가 빠르다.
- He sells cars.    그는 자동차를 판다.
- Don't spend too much money.    돈을 너무 많이 쓰지 마세요.
- He has many friends.    그는 친구들이 많아요.
- Tom is walking with the little boy.    Tom이 작은 소년과 걷고 있어요.

| **slow**<br>느린<br>[slou 슬로우] | slow　slow　slow |  |
| **buy**<br>사다, 구입하다<br>[bai 바이] | buy buy buy buy buy buy | |
| **little**<br>약간의<br>[lítl 리를] | little　little　little　little | |
| **few**<br>약간의<br>[fju: 퓨-] | few few few few few few | |
| **big**<br>큰, 커다란<br>[big 빅] | big big big big big |  |

- The turtle is slow.     거북이는 느리다.
- I buy some chocolate at the store.     나는 가게에서 초콜릿을 삽니다.
- I have a little hope.     나에게는 약간의 희망이 있어.
- Tom has a few friends.     탐에게는 친구가 몇 명 있어.
- An elephant is a big animal.     코끼리는 몸집이 큰 동물이예요.

## tall
키가 큰
[tɔːl 토-ㄹ]

tall　tall　tall　tall　tall

## left
왼쪽, 왼쪽의
[left 레프트]

left　left　left　left

## down
아래로
[daun 다운]

down　down　down　down

## under
~의 아래에
[ʌ́ndər 언덜]

under　under　under

## young
젊은, 어린
[jʌŋ 영]

young　young　young　young

| | |
|---|---|
| • He is tall. | 그는 키가 크다. |
| • Turn left there. | 저기서 왼쪽으로 도세요. |
| • I went down the stairs. | 나는 계단을 내려갔어요. |
| • There are ants under the tree. | 나무 아래 개미들이 있어요. |
| • He is young. | 그는 어리다. |

## short
짧은, 키가작은
[ʃɔːrt 쇼-ㄹ트]

short short short short

## right
오른쪽
[rait 롸잇트]

right right right

## up
위쪽으로
[ʌp 엎]

up up up up up up

## on
~의 위에
[an 언]

on on on on on on

## old
늙은
[ould 오울드]

old old old old old old

- She is **shorter** than me.   그녀는 나보다 더 작아요.
- Turn **right**.   오른쪽으로 도세요.
- Stand **up** please.   일어서 주세요.
- My pencil is **on** the desk.   책상 위에 내 연필이 있어요.
- How **old** are you?   몇 살이지요?

## true
진실의
[trú: 트루]

true true true true true

## end
끝, 마치다
[end 엔드]

end end end end end

## best
가장 좋은
[best 베스트]

best best best best

## come
오다
[kʌm 컴]

come come come come

## bright
밝은, 빛나는
[brait 브롸잇]

bright bright bright

- It is true. — 사실이야.
- This is the end. — 이것으로 끝이다.
- I did my best. — 나는 최선을 다했어요.
- Grandfather will come next Friday. — 할아버지는 다음주 금요일날 오실꺼에요.
- Look on the bright side of things. — 밝은 면을 봐(긍정적으로 생각하렴).

## false
거짓의
[fɔ́ːls 폴스]

false  false  false  false

## begin
시작하다
[bigín 비긴]

begin  begin  begin

## worst
최악의
[wə́ːrst 워어ㄹ스트]

worst  worst  worst  worst

## go
가다
[gou 고우]

go  go  go  go  go

## dark
어둠, 어두운
[daːrk 다아-ㄹ크]

dark  dark  dark  dark

- The rumor was false. 그 소문은 거짓이었어.
- Our class begins at 8. 수업은 8시에 시작한다.
- She was the worst singer. 그녀는 최악의 가수였어.
- I go to school everyday. 나는 매일 학교에 간다.
- My new skirt is dark blue. 저의 새 치마는 어두운 파란색이에요.

## far
멀리

[faːr 퐈-ㄹ]

far　far　far　far　far

## poor
가난한

[púər 푸얼]

poor poor poor poor

## start
출발하다

[staːrt 스딸-ㅌ]

start　start　start　start

## dirty
더러운, 불결한

[dɔ́ːrti 더-ㄹ리]

dirty dirty dirty dirty dirty

## in
～안에

[in 인]

in　in　in　in　in　in

- My house is far from here.    우리집은 여기서 멀어요.
- She always helps the poor.    그녀는 항상 가난한 이들을 돕는다.
- Let's start.    시작하자
- My brother's room is dirty all the time.    내 동생 방은 항상 더러워요.
- There is a cat in the box.    상자 안에 고양이 한 마리가 있다.

## near
가까운
[niər 니얼]

near near near near

## rich
돈 많은
[ritʃ 륏취]

rich rich rich rich

## stop
멈추다
[stap 스땁]

stop stop stop stop

## clean
깨끗한
[kli:n 클리인]

clean clean clean

## out
밖으로, 밖에
[aut 아웃]

out out out out out

- Our house stands near my school.
- He is very rich.
- He stopped to talk.
- I clean my room everyday.
- Let's go out.

우리집은 학교 옆에 있어요.
그는 매우 부유하다.
그는 이야기하기 위해 멈췄다.
저는 제방을 매일 청소해요.
우리 밖으로 나가자.

## push
밀다

[puʃ 푸쉬]

push　push　push　push

## strong
힘이 센, 강한

[strɔ:ŋ 스뜨뤄-엉]

strong　strong　strong

## sit
앉다

[sit 씻]

sit sit sit sit sit sit

## open
열다

[óupən 오우쁜]

open　open　open

## glad
기쁜, 반가운

[glæd 글래드]

glad　glad　glad　glad

---

- **Push** the door open.　문을 밀어서 열어요.
- The boy looks **strong**.　그 소년은 강해 보인다.
- **Sit** down, please.　앉아 주세요.
- **Open** the door, please.　문좀 열어 주세요.
- I'm **glad** to meet you.　만나서 반가워.

## pull
당기다
[pul 풀]

pull　pull　pull　pull

## weak
약한
[wíːk 위-크]

weak　weak　weak　weak

## stand
서다, 일어서다
[stænd 스땐드]

stand　stand　stand　stand

## shut
닫다, 덮다
[ʃʌt 셧]

shut shut shut shut shut

## sad
슬 픈
[sǽd 쌔에드]

sad　sad　sad　sad

- **Pull** the door open. — 문을 당겨서 열어요.
- Tom is **weak**. — Tom은 (체력이)약해요.
- **Stand** up, please. — 일어서 주세요.
- Please **shut** the window. — 창문 좀 닫아 주세요.
- She looks **sad**. — 그녀는 슬퍼보여.

## high
높은

[hái 하이]

high high high high

## great
큰, 엄청난

[greit 그뤠잇]

great great great great

## wide
넓은

[waid 와이드]

wide wide wide

## fine
좋은

[fain 퐈인]

fine fine fine fine fine fine

## warm
따뜻한

[wɔːrm 워-ㄹ엄]

warm warm warm

- Mt. Everest is really high.
- I heard some great news!
- That place is wide.
- The weather is fine, today.
- Today is warm.

에베레스트 산은 정말 높아요.
나 엄청난 소식을 들었어!
그곳은 넓어요.
오늘 날씨가 좋아요.
오늘은 따뜻하다.

| **low**<br>낮은<br>[lóu 로우] | low low low low low |
| **little**<br>작은<br>[lítl 리를] | little little little little little |
| **narrow**<br>좁은<br>[nǽrou 내로오우] | narrow narrow narrow |
| **bad**<br>나쁜<br>[bǽd 베드] | bad bad bad bad  |
| **cold**<br>추운<br>[kóuld 코울드] | cold cold cold cold  |

- The temperature is low today.  오늘은 기온이 낮다.
- You just look like a little kid.  넌 그냥 어린 애처럼 보여.
- He jumped a narrow stream.  그는 좁은 개울을 뛰어넘었어.
- I feel bad today.  난 오늘 기분이 나빠.
- It's cold in winter.  겨울은 추워요.

## long
긴

[lɔːŋ 러-엉]

long long long long

## lot
많음

[lat 랏]

lot lot lot lot lot lot

## hate
싫어하다

[heit 헤잇트]

hate hate hate hate

## hot
더운, 뜨거운

[hat 핫]

hot hot hot hot hot hot

## easy
쉬운

[íːzi 이-지]

easy easy easy easy

- A giraffe has a long neck.
- There are a lot of people on the beach.
- I hate mouse.
- I don't like hot weather.
- It's easy to say "Thank you."

기린은 목이 길어요.
해변에 사람이 많아요.
난 쥐를 싫어해.
나는 더운 날씨를 별로 안 좋아해요.
고맙다고 말하는 건 쉬워요.

| **short**<br>짧은<br>[ʃɔ́:rt 쇼올트] | short   short   short | 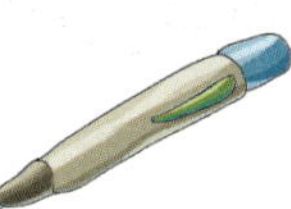 |

| **few**<br>거의 없는<br>[fjú: 퓨] | few few few few few few |

| **like**<br>좋아하다<br>[láik 라익] | like   like   like   like   like |

| **cool**<br>시원한<br>[kú:l 쿠울] | cool cool cool cool |  |

| **difficult**<br>어려운<br>[dífikʌ̀lt 디퓌컬트] | difficult   difficult   difficult |

- She likes to wear short skirt.
- I have few books.
- Sally likes you.
- I want to drink cool water.
- That is so difficult problem to solve.

그녀는 짧은 치마 입는 것을 좋아해.
나는 책이 거의 없어.
셀리가 널 좋아해.
나 시원한 물이 마시고 싶어.
저건 풀기에 너무 어려운 문제야.

# behind
시작하다
[biháind 비하인드]

behind   behind   behind

# into
~안으로
[intu 인투]

into into into into into into

# happy
행복한
[hǽpi 해삐]

happy happy happy

# equal
같은
[íːkwəl 이쿠얼]

equal   equal   equal   equal

- Tom smiles behind Merry.    수업은 8시에 시작한다.
- Jim went into his house.    Jim은 그의 집으로 들어갔어요.
- I'm happy to be with you.    너랑 있어 행복해.
- Ducks are equal in size.    오리들은 크기가 같다.

## ahead
앞쪽에
[əhéd 어헤드]

ahead   ahead   ahead

## outside
밖에
[áutsáid 아웃사이드]

outside   outside

## unhappy
불행한
[ʌ́nhǽpi 언해삐]

unhappy   unhappy

## different
다른
[dífərənt 디퍼런트]

different   different

---

- She went **ahead** of me.     그녀는 나를 앞서갔다.
- It's a lovely day **outside**.     밖에 날씨가 너무 좋아요.
- She was **unhappy** about the news.     그녀는 그 소식에 슬픈 생각이 들었다.
- I need a **different** pen.     나 다른 펜이 필요해.

## deep
깊은

[diːp 디-입]

deep deep deep

## take
받다

[teik 테익]

take take take take take

## fast
빠른

[fæst 페스트]

fast fast fast fast

## cheap
값이 싼, 싸게

[tʃiːp 취-입]

cheap cheap cheap cheap

---

- How deep is the river?    강이 얼마나 깊나요?
- Take this letter to your mother.    이 편지를 어머니께 가져다 드리렴.
- It is very fast train.    이건 굉장히 빠른 기차예요.
- The candy was very cheap.    그 사탕은 값이 쌌어요.

| **low** | low low low low low low |
| 얕은 | |
| [lóu 로우] | |

| **give** | give give give |
| 주다 | |
| [gív 기브] |  |

| **slow** | slow slow slow slow slow |
| 느린 | |
| [slóu 슬로우] | |

| **expensive** | expensive        expensive |
| 비싼 | |
| [ikspénsiv 익스펜시브] | |

- The stream was so low that we could cross it. — 개울가가 얕아서 우리가 건널 수 있었다.
- Please, give me that book. — 그 책을 좀 줘.
- Will you slow down? — 좀 천천히 할래?
- Isn't this pretty expensive? — 이거 꽤 비싸지 않아?

# 15. 움직임을 나타내는 단어

**act**
행동하다
[ækt 액트]

act act act act act act

**appear**
나타나다
[əpíər 어피얼]

appear appear appear

**arrive**
도착하다
[əráiv 어롸이브]

arrive arrive arrive

**bear**(2)
낳다
[bɛər 베어-ㄹ]

bear bear bear bear

- He acts like a father.　　그는 아빠인 것처럼 행동한다.
- He appears in the room.　　그가 방에 나타났다(들어왔다).
- Dad will arrive soon.　　도착하실꺼야.
- Dogs usually bear four puppies.　　개는 보통 4마리의 새끼를 낳는다.

| **become** ~이 되다 <br> [bikʌ́m 비컴] | become become become |
| --- | --- |
| **blow** 불다 <br> [blou 블로우] | blow blow blow blow blow |
| **break** 부수다 <br> [breik브뤠익크] | break break break break |
| **bring** 가져오다 <br> [briŋ 브룅] | bring bring bring  |
| **broke** 깨트렸다 <br> [brouk브로-크] | broke broke broke broke |

- Hungbu **became** the rich man.
- My father is **blowing** up balloons.
- A glass is easy to **break**.
- **Bring** me the book, please.
- I **broke** my grandma's glasses.

홍부는 부자가 되었어요.
아빠가 풍선을 불고 계셔요.
유리는 깨지기 쉽다.
그 책 좀 가져다 주렴.
내가 할머니의 안경을 깨뜨렸다.

| | |
|---|---|
| **build** <br> 세우다, 짓다 <br> [bild 빌드] | build build build build |
| **burn** <br> 타다, 태우다 <br> [bəːrn 버−ㄹ언] | burn burn burn burn |
| **call** <br> 부르다 <br> [kɔːl 커얼] | call call call call   |
| **carry** <br> 운반하다 <br> [kǽri 캐뤼] | carry carry carry carry |
| **catch** <br> 잡다, 받다 <br> [kætʃ 캣취] | catch catch catch catch |

- I want to **build** a doghouse.    나는 개집을 짓고 싶어요.
- Mom **burned** the steaks today.    엄마는 오늘 스테이크를 태웠어요.
- My friends **call** me Sunny.    친구들은 저를 Sunny라고 불러요.
- I always **carry** schoolbag.    저는 항상 책가방을 가지고 다녀요.
- Cats are very good at **catching** mice.    고양이는 쥐를 아주 잘 잡아요.

## close
닫다
[klouz 클로우즈]

close close close close

## could
can의 과거형
[kud 쿠드]

could could could could

## count
수를 세다
[kaunt 카운트]

count count count count

## cross
가로지르다
[crɔːs 크뤄스]

cross cross cross cross

## cry
소리치다, 울다
[krai 크롸이]

cry cry cry cry

- Close one eye and look at that.   한쪽 눈을 감고 저것을 봐봐.
- I could carry the box.   나는 그 상자를 옮길 수 있었어요.
- Let's count to 10! 1, 2, 3...   10까지 세어보자! 일, 이, 삼...
- Let's cross the street.   길을 건너자.
- "Why are you crying?"   왜 울고 있니?

## cut
베다, 깎다
[kʌt 컷]

cut cut cut cut cut

## die
죽다
[dai 다이]

die die die die die die

## drink
마시다
[driŋk 쥬륑크]

drink drink drink

## drive
운전하다
[draiv 드롸이브]

drive drive drive

## drop
떨어뜨리다
[drap 드롸ㅂ]

drop drop drop drop

---

- I had cut my finger.    나는 손가락을 베었다.
- That sick dog will die.    저 아픈 개는 죽을거야.
- If you are thirsty, drink some water.    목이 마르면 물을 좀 마시세요.
- Can you drive a car?    차 운전할 줄 알아요?
- "Don't drop the dishes."    접시 떨어뜨리지 마라.

## eat
먹다

[iːt 이-잇]

eat　eat　eat　eat

## enjoy
즐기다

[éndʒɔ́i엔쵀이]

enjoy　enjoy　enjoy

## excite
흥분시키다

[iksáit익씨이트]

excite　excite　excite　excite

## excuse
용서하다

[ikskjúːz익스큐즈]

excuse　excuse　excuse

## feel
느끼다

[fiːl 퓌-일]

feel　feel　feel　feel　feel

---

- I like to eat salads.　　샐러드는 먹는 걸 좋아해요.
- My dad enjoys driving.　　아빠는 운전을 즐기셔요.
- The game excited us.　　그 시합은 우리를 흥분시켰다.
- Excuse me.　　실례합니다.
- I feel the summer is coming.　　여름이 오고있는게 느껴져요.

## fight
싸우다

[fait 파잇트]

fight   fight   fight   fight

## fill
채우다

[fil 필]

fill   fill   fill   fill   fill

## find
찾다, 발견하다

[faind 파인드]

find   find   find   find   find

## finish
끝내다, 마치다

[fíniʃ 퓌니쉬]

finish   finish   finish   finish

## fix
수리하다

[fiks 퓌ㄱ스]

fix   fix   fix   fix   fix   fix

---

- Sometimes I fight with my brother.    가끔 동생이랑 싸워요.
- Fill in the blank.    빈칸을 채우세요.
- I can't find my doll.    제 인형을 찾을 수가 없어요.
- Let's finish it today.    오늘 그걸 끝냅시다.
- Dad and I will fix the roof today.    아빠랑 오늘 지붕을 고칠꺼에요.

## fly (1)
날다

[flai 플롸이]

fly　fly　fly　fly　fly

## follow
따르다

[fálou퐈ㄹ로우]

follow follow follow follow

## forget
잊다

[fərgét 폴겟]

forget forget forget forget

## happen
발생하다

[hǽpən 해쁜]

happen　happen　happen

## have
가지고 있다

[hæv 해브]

have　have　have

- I can't fly.
- "Where is the hospital?" "Follow me"
- Did you forget to buy some apples?
- How did it happen?
- I have a lot of stamps.

나는 날 수 없어요.
"병원이 어디있나요" "저를 따라 오세요"
사과 사는 거 잊으셨어요?
어떻게 그 일이 발생했나요?
저는 우표를 아주 많이 가지고 있어요.

## help
돕다
[help 헬-프]

help help help help

## hit
때리다
[hit 힛]

hit hit hit hit hit hit

## hide
숨기다, 숨다
[haid 하이드]

hide hide hide hide

## hold
잡다, 붙들다
[hould 호울드]

hold hold hold hold hold

## hope
바라다
[houp 호웁]

hope hope hope hope

- **Help** me, please! — 저를 도와주세요!
- Don't **hit** me! — 나를 때리지 마.
- Don't **hide** my doll. — 내 인형 숨기지마!!
- "**Hold** my hand!", he cries. — "내 손을 잡아!" 그가 외쳤어요.
- I **hope** you have a good time. — 좋은 시간되시길 바랍니다.

## hurry
서두르다
[həːri 허-뤼]

hurry hurry hurry hurry

## hurt
다치게 하다
[həːrt 허-르트]

hurt hurt hurt hurt hurt

## keep
계속하다
[kiːp 키-입]

keep keep keep keep

## kick
차다
[kik 킥]

kick kick kick kick

## kill
죽이다, 없애다
[kil 킬]

kill kill kill kill kill kill

- Hurry up, or we'll be late.　서둘러! 안 그러면 늦을꺼야.
- I am badly hurt.　난 심하게 다쳤어요.
- Keep your room clean.　당신의 방을 깨끗히 유지하세요.
- Tom kicked a ball.　Tom은 공을 찼어요.
- Cats kill the mouse.　고양이는 쥐를 죽여요.

## knock
두드리다

[nak 낙]

knock  knock  knock

## know
알다, 이해하다

[nou 노우]

know  know  know  know

## jump
뛰어오르다

[dʒʌmp 줘ㅁ프]

jump  jump  jump

## laugh
웃다

[læf 래프]

laugh  laugh  laugh  laugh

## let
시키다

[let 렛]

let  let  let  let  let  let

---

- I **knocked** the door.
- Do you **know** what I mean?
- Teddy is ready to **jump** up.
- He **laughs** loudly.
- I **let** him go out.

전 노크를 했어요.
내가 무슨 말 하는 지 알겠어?
Teddy는 뛰어오를 준비가 되었어요
그는 큰 소리로 웃었어요.
그를 나가게 했어요.

## leave
떠나다
[liːv 리-브]

leave leave leave

## like
좋아하다
[laik 라이크]

like like like like like

## look
보다
[luk 룩]

look look look

## love
사랑하다
[lʌv 러브]

love love love love love

## make
만들다
[meik 메이크]

make make make make

---

- I **leave** at 3.
- I **like** dancing.
- **Look** at it. Do you know what it is?
- Mom and dad **love** each other.
- I **made** a cake for my mother.

나는 3시에 떠나요.
저는 춤추는 걸 좋아해요.
이것 좀 봐. 이게 뭔지 알아?
엄마 아빠는 서로를 사랑하셔요.
나는 어머니를 위해 케이크를 만들었어요.

**may**
~해도 좋다
[mei 메이]

may　may　may　may

**meet**
만나다
[miːt 미잇트]

meet　meet　meet

**move**
움직이다
[muːv 무-브]

move　move　move　move

**must**
꼭 해야만 한다
[mʌst 머스트]

must　must　must　must

**pass**
지나가다
[pæs 패스]

pass　pass　pass　pass

- You **may** go now.　넌 이제 가도 좋다.
- I am glad to **meet** you.　만나게 되어서 기뻐요.
- We **moved** to a new house.　우리는 새집으로 이사했어요.
- You **must** do this.　당신은 이것을 해야만 한다.
- I **passed** through the park.　나는 공원을 가로질러 지나갔다.

| **pick**<br>따다<br>[pik 픽] | pick   pick   pick   pick   pick |
| **play**<br>연주하다, 놀다<br>[plei 플레이] | play   play   play   play  |
| **please**<br>기쁘게 하다<br>[pliːz플리이즈] | please please please  |
| **put**<br>놓다, 두다<br>[put 풋] | put   put   put   put   put |
| **ran**<br>달렸다<br>[ræn 뤤] | ran   ran   ran   ran   ran |

- Please, pick one of them.  그것들 중 하나를 고르세요.
- She plays the violin very well.  그녀는 바이올린 연주를 매우 잘한다.
- I am pleased to see you.  너를 보게 되어 기뻐.
- I put some flowers into the vase.  꽃병에 꽃 몇 송이를 넣었다.
- Tiger ran fast.  호랑이는 빨리 달렸다.

| **record** 기록하다 [rikɔ́ːrd 뢰커-ㄹ드] | record　　record　　record |
| **remember** 기억하다 [rimémbər 뤼멤버얼] | remember　　remember |
| **ride** 타다 [raid 롸이드] | ride　ride　ride　ride　ride |
| **ring** 울리다 [riŋ 륑] | ring　ring　ring　ring　ring |
| **run** 달리다 [rʌn 뤄ㄴ] | run run run run run  |

- I record everything in this note.　나는 모든 것을 이 노트에 기록한다.
- I remember her.　나는 그녀를 기억한다.
- Can you ride a bicycle?　자전거 탈 줄 아니?
- The telephone is ringing.　전화가 울리고 있어요.
- I like to run.　나는 달리는 걸 좋아해요.

## see
보다

[siː 씨-]

see  see  see  see

## send
보내다

[send 쎈드]

send  send  send  send

## shall
~일 것이다

[ʃæl 셸]

shall  shall  shall  shall

## shoot
쏘다, 던지다

[ʃuːt 슛]

shoot  shoot  shoot  shoot

## shout
소리치다

[ʃaut 샤웃]

shout  shout  shout  shout

- I want to see you!    네가 보고싶어!
- I will send you an e-mail.    나는 너에게 e-mail을 보낼 것이다.
- I shall be very happy to see you.    너를 보게 되면 매우 기쁠 거야.
- He tried to shoot a bird.    그는 새 한 마리를 쏘려고 하였다.
- Don't shout to your brother.    동생에게 소리치지 마라.

| **show** 보이다 [ʃou 쇼우] | show　show　show　show |
| **slide** 미끄러지다 [slaid슬라이드] | slide slide slide slide slide |
| **smell** 냄새맡다 [smel 스멜] | smell　smell　smell　smell |
| **smile** 웃다, 미소지다 [smail 스마일] | smile　smile　smile |
| **spend** 낭비하다 [spend 스뺀드] | spend spend spend spend |

- Can you **show** it to me? — 그것을 내게 보여줄 수 있니?
- She **slid** on the ice. — 그녀는 얼음판 위에서 미끄러졌다.
- It **smells** good. — 좋은 냄새가 난다.
- She **smiled** at me. — 그녀가 나를 보고 웃었다.
- How much money do you **spend**? — 돈을 얼마나 썼니?

## strike
때리다

[straik스뜨롸익]

strike strike strike strike

## taste
맛을 보다

[teist테이스트]

taste taste taste taste

## throw
던지다

[θrou 쓰로우]

throw throw throw throw

## wait
기다리다

[weit 웨잇]

wait wait wait wait wait

## walk
걷다, 산책하다

[wɔːk 워-억]

walk walk walk

- I strike a ball.
- It tastes sweet.
- The pitcher threw a ball to me.
- Min-ho is waiting for his girl friend.
- I walk in the park with my wife everyday.

나는 공을 친다.
단맛이 난다.
투수가 나에게 공을 던졌어요.
민호는 그의 여자 친구를 기다립니다.
나는 매일 아내와 공원을 걷는다.

# 16. 모양이나 상태를 나타내는 단어

**afraid**
무서워하여
[əfréid 어프뢰이드]

afraid afraid afraid afraid

**angry**
화난
[ǽŋgri 앵그뤼]

angry angry angry

**any**
무엇이든
[éni 애니]

any any any any any

**beautiful**
아름다운
[bjú:təfəl 뷰-러플]

beautiful beautiful

- I'm much afraid of snakes.　　나는 뱀이 아주 무서워요.
- Tom looks angry.　　Tom이 화난 것 같아.
- Do you have any questions?　　무슨 질문이 있나요?
- Snow white is beautiful.　　백설공주는 예뻐요.

## broken
부러진
[broukən 브뤄큰]

broken   broken   broken

## busy
바쁜
[bízì 비지]

busy   busy   busy

## careful
조심스러운
[kɛərfəl 캐어ㄹ풀]

careful   careful   careful

## close
가까운, 친한
[klous 클로우즈]

close   close   close   close

## dead
죽은
[ded 데드]

dead   dead   dead   dead

---

- My left arm was broken.     내 왼쪽 팔이 부러졌다.
- My parents are busy.     우리 부모님은 바쁘셔요.
- Be careful not to drop the cup.     컵을 떨어뜨리지 않게 조심해.
- Tom and Jerry are very close friends.     Tom과 Jerry는 아주 친한 친구 사이예요.
- My cat was dead.     제 고양이가 죽었어요.

# empty
텅 빈
[émpti 엠프티]

empty empty empty

# enough
충분한
[inʌ́f 이너프]

enough enough enough

# every
모든
[évriː 에브뤼]

every every every

# fair
공평한, 공정한
[fɛər 페얼]

fair fair fair fair fair fair

# few
거의 없는
[fjuː 퓨－]

few few few few few few

| | |
|---|---|
| · The room is empty. | 그 방은 비었어요. |
| · I think that's enough. | 그거면 충분하다고 생각해. |
| · Everyone likes him. | 모두 그를 좋아해요. |
| · I think it was a fair game. | 공정한 게임이었다고 생각해요. |
| · I have few cards. | 나는 카드도 별로 없어요. |

## foolish
어리석은

[fúːliʃ 푸-울리쉬]

foolish foolish foolish

## free
자유로운

[friː 프뤼-]

free free free free free

## fresh
새로운, 신선한

[freʃ 프뤗쉬]

fresh fresh fresh fresh

## full
가득한, 충만한

[ful 풀]

full full full full

## good
좋은, 착한

[gud 굿]

good good good good

- It was a foolish idea.
- What do you do in your free time?
- These vegetables look fresh.
- The box is full of books.
- I think it is a good idea.

그건 어리석은 생각이었어요.
한가할 때 뭐하세요?
이 야채들은 신선해 보여요.
이 박스에는 책이 가득 들어있다.
좋은 생각인 것 같아요.

# hard
딱딱한, 어려운

[haːrd 하알드]

hard   hard   hard   hard

# hungry
배고픈

[hʌ́ŋgri 헝그뤼]

hungry   hungry

# ill
아픈, 병든

[il 일]

ill ill ill ill ill ill

# kind
친절한

[kaind 카인드]

kind kind kind kind kind

# late
늦은, 늦게

[leit 레잇]

late late late late late

---

- It is very hard to solve this problem.   이 문제를 해결하는 건 어려워요.
- I'm very hungry.   나 정말 배고파요.
- Teddy is ill in bed.   Teddy는 아파서 누워있어요.
- The police officer is very kind.   그 경찰관은 매우 친절해요.
- Let's meet at 7 o'clock. Don't be late.   7시에 만나자. 늦지마!

## lonely
외로운
[lóunlí 로운리]

lonely lonely lonely lonely

## loud
목소리가 큰
[laud 라우드]

loud loud loud loud loud

## mad
미친, 열광한
[mæd 매드]

mad mad mad mad

## new
새로운
[njuː 뉴-]

new new new new

## next
다음의, 다음에
[nekst 넥스트]

next next next next next

- I feel lonely. / 나는 외롭다.
- He has a loud voice. / 그는 목소리가 커요.
- He is mad about games. / 그는 게임에 열중해 있다.
- I wear a new uniform. / 나는 새로운 교복을 입는다.
- See you next time. / 다음에 보자.

## nice
멋진
[nais 나이스]

nice　nice　nice　nice

## no
하나도 없는
[nóu 노우]

no　no　no　no　no　no

## only
오직, 유일한
[óunli 오운리]

only　only　only　only　only

## poor
가난한, 불쌍한
[puər 푸얼]

poor　poor　poor

## quiet
조용한
[kwáiət콰이엇-ㅌ]

quiet　quiet　quiet

- This jacket is very nice. — 이 자켓은 매우 멋져요.
- There are no one in the room. — 방엔 아무도 없어요.
- She is an only daughter. — 그녀는 외동딸이야.
- He is a poor man. — 그는 불쌍한 사람이다.
- Be quiet! — 조용히 해!

## ready
준비가 된
[rédi 뢰디]

ready ready ready

## round
둥근, 동그란
[raund 롸운드]

round round round round

## sad
슬픈, 슬퍼하는
[sæd 쌔드]

sad sad sad sad

## safe
안전한
[seif 쎄이프]

safe safe safe safe safe

## same
동일한, 똑같은
[seim 쎄임]

same same same same

- Are you ready to order? — 주문할 준비 되셨어요?
- There is a round table. — 거기 둥근 탁자가 있다.
- I am very sad. — 나는 매우 슬퍼요.
- There is a safe place. — 안전한 장소다.
- We have the same caps. — 우리는 똑같은 모자를 가지고 있다.

# sick
아픈, 병든

[sik 씩]

sick sick sick sick sick

# sorry
죄송한

[sɔ́ːri 써-뤼]

sorry sorry sorry sorry

# stupid
어리석은

[stjúːpid 스뚜피-드]

stupid stupid stupid stupid

# thank
감사하다

[θæŋk 쌩크]

thank thank thank

# wet
젖은, 축축한

[wet 웨트]

wet wet wet wet

- My grandmother is sick.     할머니가 아프시다.
- I am sorry to hear that.     그것 참 유감이에요.
- He is stupid.     그는 어리석다.
- Thank you very much.     정말 감사합니다.
- We have the wet season in June.     6월은 장마철이다.

# 17. 부 사

**ago**
~전에
[əgóu 어고우]

ago    ago    ago    ago    ago

**again**
다시, 또
[əgén 어게인]

again    again    again    again

**also**
역시, 또한
[ɔ́:lsou 오–올쏘우]

also    also    also    also    also

**always**
항상, 언제나
[ɔ́:lweiz 어–얼웨이즈]

always    always

- I met him three years ago.     3년 전에 그를 만났다.
- Do it again.     다시 해 보렴.
- Tom is kind, also handsome.     Tom은 착하고, 또한 잘 생겼다.
- Mike is always late.     Mike는 항상 늦는다.

## around
~의 주위에
[əráund 어롸운드]

around　around　around

## early
이른, 일찍
[ə́ːrli 이-ㄹ리]

early　early　early

## else
그밖에
[els 엘스]

else　else　else　else　else

## ever
이제까지
[évər 에벌]

ever　ever　ever　ever　ever

## just
방금, 오직
[dʒʌst 줘스트]

just　just　just　just　just

- I looked around the village.   저는 마을 주위를 둘러보았어요.
- I get up early in the morning.   나는 아침 일찍 일어나요.
- "Anything else?"   그 밖의 다른 것은요?
- "Have you ever heard the song?"   그 노래 들어봤니?
- I just arrived here.   저는 방금 여기에 도착했어요.

## last
마지막으로
[læst 래스트]

last last last last last

## not
아니다, 않다
[nat 낫]

not not not not not not

## now
지금, 방금
[nau 나우]

now now now now

## off
~떨어져
[ɔːf 어프]

off off off off off 

## so
정말로, 그렇게
[sou 쏘우]

so so so so so so so so so

- When did you see him last?
- Is it a cat? No, It is not.
- It is over now.
- Don't take off your shoes.
- You must not behave so.

마지막으로 그를 본 게 언제였죠?
그것은 고양이입니다? 그것은 고양이가 아닙니다.
이제 끝났다.
신발 벗지 마세요.
그렇게 행동해서는 안된다.

## soon
곧
[suːn 쑤-운]

soon　soon　soon　soon

## then
그 때, 그러면
[ðen 덴]

then　then　then　then　then

## too
~도 또한
[tuː 튜-]

too　too　too　too　too

## very
매우, 아주
[véri 붸뤼]

very　very　very

## well
만족하게, 잘
[wel 웰]

well　well　well　well

- See you soon. — 곧 보자!
- Father was a little child then. — 그 당시 아버지는 작은 어린아이였다.
- Me, too. — 나 또한 그래.
- I like it very much. — 난 그것을 매우 좋아해요.
- He speaks English very well. — 그는 영어를 아주 잘한다.

# 18. 전치사

**about**
약, 거의
[əbáut 어바웃]

about  about  about  about

**across**
~의 건너편
[əkrɔ́ːs 어크뤄-스]

across    across    across

**after**
~후에
[ǽftər 애프터ㄹ]

after    after    after

**along**
~따라서
[əlɔ́ːŋ 얼러엉]

along  along  along  along

- What is the book about? | 이 책은 무엇에 관한 내용이야?
- My house is across from the park. | 우리집은 공원 건너편에 있어요.
- Please repeat after me. | 제가 말한 후에 따라하세요(제 말을 따라하세요).
- Amy walked along the street. | Amy는 길을 따라 걸었다.

# among
~의 사이에

[əmʌ́ŋ 어멍]

among　among　among

# as
~만큼

[æz 애즈]

as　as　as　as　as　as　as　as

# at
~에서

[æt 앳]

at　at　at　at　at　at

# below
~보다 아래에

[bilóu 빌로우]

below　below　below

# beside
~의 곁에

[bisáid 비싸이드]

beside　beside　beside

- The car is among the trees.
- Tom is as tall as I am.
- I study at home.
- Cat is below the table.
- Tom is standing beside his friends.

차가 나무들 사이에 있다.
Tom은 나와 키가 같다(톰은 나와 같은 정도의 키다).
나는 집에서 공부한다.
탁자 아래 고양이가 있어요.
Tom은 친구들 옆에 서 있다.

## by
곁에, ~로써
[bai 바이]

by　by　by　by　by　by

## children
child의 복수형
[tʃíldrən 칠드런]

children　children　children

## for
~을 위해서
[fɔːr 포-ㄹ]

for　for　for　for　for　for

## from
~에서
[frʌm 프럼]

from from from from from

## if
(만약)~라면
[if 이프]

if  if  if  if  if  if  if

- I go to school by bus. — 나는 버스 타고(버스로) 학교 가요.
- There are a lot of children on the ground. — 운동장에 아이들이 많아요.
- This is for you. — 이것은 너를 위한 거야.
- I'm from Japan. — 저는 일본에서 왔어요.
- If I were you, I would do my best. — (만약)내가 너라면, 난 최선을 다할텐데.

# 찾아보기

## a

a 하나의, 한사람의(76)
about 약, 거의(145)
across ~의 건너편(145)
act 행동하다(114)
afraid 무서워하여(132)
after ~후에(145)
afternoon 오후(72)
again 다시, 또(141)
age 나이(76)
ago ~전에(141)
ahead 앞쪽에(111)
air 공기(86)
airplane 비행기(56)
airport 공항(58)
album 앨범, 사진첩(44)
along ~따라서(145)
also 역시, 또한(141)
always 항상, 언제나(141)
am ~이다(69)
ambulance 구급차(56)
among ~의 사이에(146)
an 하나의(77)
and 그리고, ~와(63)
angry 화난(132)
animal 동물, 짐승(81)
ant 개미(81)
any 무엇이든(132)
apartment 아파트(18)
appear 나타나다(114)
apple 사과(36)
April 4월(72)
are ~이다(70)
arm 팔(10)
around ~의 주위에(142)
arrive 도착하다(114)
art 미술, 예술(27)
as ~만큼(146)
ask 묻다, 질문하다(63)
at ~에서(146)
aunt 아주머니, 이모(54)
autumn 가을(72)

## b

baby 아기(54)
bad 나쁜(107)
bag 가방, 봉지(44)
ball 공(27)
ballon 풍선(51)
banana 바나나(36)
bank 은행(58)
basket 바구니(18)
be ~이다(70)
beach 물가, 바닷가(86)
bear(1) 곰(81)
bear(2) 낳다(114)
beautiful 아름다운(132)
because 왜냐하면(63)
become ~이 되다(115)
bed 침대(18)
begin 시작하다(101)
behind 뒤에(110)
bell 종, 초인종(18)
below ~보다 아래에(146)
bench 긴 의자, 벤치(19)
beside ~의 곁에(146)
best 가장 좋은(100)
bicycle 자전거(56)
big 큰, 커다란(97)
bird 새(81)
birthday 생일(24)
black 검은 색(51)
blow 불다(115)
blue 파란색(51)
board 판자, 게시판(44)
boat 보트, 작은배(56)
body 몸, 신체(10)
book 책(44)
boy 소년(54)
bread 빵(32)
break 부수다(115)
breakfast 아침식사(32)
bridge 다리(59)
bright 밝은, 빛나는(100)
bring 가져오다(115)
broke 깨트렸다(115)
broken 부러진(133)
brother 형제(24)
brown 갈색, 갈색의(51)
build 세우다, 짓다(116)
burn 타다, 태우다(116)
bus 버스(57)
busy 바쁜(133)
but 그러나, 하지만(63)
butter 버터(32)
button 단추, 버튼(14)
buy 사다, 구입하다(97)
by 곁에, ~로써(147)
bye (헤어질 때)안녕(64)

## c

cake 케이크(32)
calendar 달력(72)
call 부르다(116)
camera 카메라(27)
camp 캠프(45)
candy 사탕(33)
cap 모자(14)
capital 수도, 서울(59)
captain 선장, 우두머리(38)
car 자동차(57)
careful 조심스러운(133)
carry 운반하다(116)
cat 고양이(82)
catch 잡다, 받다(116)
chair 의자(19)
chalk 분필(45)
cheap 값이 싼, 싸게(112)
cheese 치즈(33)
chicken 닭(82)
child 어린이(54)
children child의 복수형(147)
church 교회(59)
city 도시(59)
class 수업, 학급(45)
clean 깨끗한(103)
close 닫다(117)
close 가까운, 친한(133)
clothes 옷(14)
cloud 구름(86)
club 클럽, 동호회(27)
coat 외투(14)
coffee 커피(33)
coin 동전(49)
cold 추운(107)
color 색깔(52)
come 오다(100)
computer 컴퓨터(45)
cook 요리사(38)
cool 시원한(109)
corn 옥수수(36)
could can의 과거형(117)
count 수를 세다(117)
country 나라, 지역(86)
course 진로, 과정(39)
cousin 사촌, 친척(24)
cow 암소, 젖소(82)
crayon 크레용(45)
cream 크림(33)
cross 가로지르다(117)
cry 소리치다, 울다(117)
cucumber 오이(36)
cup 컵(19)
curtain 커튼(19)
cut 베다, 깎다(118)

## d

dad 아빠(24)
dance 춤, 춤추다(28)
dark 어둠, 어두운(101)
date 날짜(73)
daughter 딸(25)
day 낮, 하루(73)
dead 죽은(133)
deep 깊은(112)
deer 사슴(82)
desk 책상(46)
dictionary 사전(64)
did 했다, 했었다(70)
die 죽다(118)
dinner 저녁 식사(33)
dirty 더러운, 불결한(102)
dish 접시(19)
do 하다(70)
doctor 의사(38)
does do의 3인칭 단수(71)
dog 개(82)
doll 인형(52)
dollar 달러(49)
door 문(20)
down 아래로(98)
dress 의복(14)
drink 마시다(118)
drive 운전하다(118)
drop 떨어뜨리다(118)
drum 북, 드럼(28)
dry 마른(??)
duck 오리(83)

## e

ear 귀(10)
early 이른, 일찍(142)
earth 지구, 땅(87)
east 동쪽(79)
easy 쉬운(108)
eat 먹다(119)
egg 달걀(34)
elephant 코끼리(83)
else 그밖에(142)
empty 텅 빈(134)
end 끝, 마치다(100)
enjoy 즐기다(119)

enough 충분한(134)
equal 같은(110)
eraser 지우개(46)
evening 저녁(73)
ever 이제까지(142)
every 모든(134)
example 보기, 예(64)
excite 흥분시키다(119)
excuse 용서하다(119)
exercise 운동, 연습(28)
eye 눈(11)

## f

face 얼굴(11)
fair 공평한, 공정한(134)
fall 가을(73)
false 거짓의(101)
family 가족(25)
far 멀리(102)
fast 빠른(112)
fat 뚱뚱한(94)
father 아버지(25)
feel 느끼다(119)
few 거의 없는(109,97,134)
field 들판(87)
fight 싸우다(120)
fill 채우다(120)
film 필름, 영화(28)
find 찾다, 발견하다(120)
fine 좋은(106)
finger 손가락(11)
finish 끝내다, 마치다(120)
fish 물고기(84)
fix 수리하다(120)
floor 바닥, 층(59)
fly⁽¹⁾ 날다(121)
fly⁽²⁾ 파리(83)
follow 따르다(121)
food 음식(34)
foolish 어리석은(135)
foot 발(11)
for ~을 위해서(147)
forget 잊다(121)
fork 포크(20)
free 자유로운(135)
fresh 새로운, 신선한(135)
four 4, 4의(77)
fox 여우(83)
friend 친구(54)

from ~에서(147)
fruit 과일(37)
full 가득한, 충만한(135)

## g

game 게임·놀이(28)
garden 정원(20)
gas 가스(20)
gate 문, 출입구(60)
girl 소녀(55)
give 주다(113)
glad 기쁜, 반가운(104)
glass 유리, 유리컵(20)
glove 장갑(15)
go 가다(101)
god 하느님(39)
gold 금(87)
good 좋은, 착한(135)
grandmother 할머니(25)
grape 포도(37)
grass 풀(87)
gray 회색, 회색의(52)
great 큰, 엄청난(106)
green 녹색(87)
ground 땅, 운동장(88)
group 무리, 모임, 떼(40)
guitar 기타(29)

## h

hair 머리카락, 털(77,11)
hamburger 햄버거(32)
hand 손(12)
happen 발생하다(121)
happy 행복한(110)
hard 딱딱한, 어려운(136)
hat 모자(15)
hate 싫어하다(108)
have 가지고 있다(121)
he 그는, 그가(5)
head 머리(12)
hear 듣다(64)
heart 마음, 심장(12)
heavy 무거운(94)
hello 안녕, 여보세요(64)
help 돕다(122)
hen 암탉(84)
her 그녀의(6)

hers 그녀의 것(9)
hide 숨기다, 숨다(122)
high 높은(106)
hill 언덕(88)
him 그를, 그에게(5)
his 그의, 그의 것(5)
hit 때리다(122)
hold 잡다, 붙들다(122)
holiday 휴일, 공휴일(73)
home 집(21)
hope 바라다(122)
horse 말(84)
hospital 병원(60)
hot 더운, 뜨거운(108)
hotel 호텔(60)
hour 시간(77)
house 집(21)
how 어떻게, 얼마나(65)
hundred 백(100)(77)
hungry 배고픈(136)
hurry 서두르다(123)
hurt 다치게 하다(123)

## i

I 나는, 내가(4)
ice 얼음(88)
idea 생각(65)
if (만약)~라면(147)
ill 아픈, 병든(136)
in ~안에(102)
ink 잉크(46)
into ~안으로(110)
is ~에 있다(71)
island 섬(88)
it 그것은(6)
its 그것의(6)

## j

job 일, 직업(38)
Juice 주스(34)
jump 뛰어오르다(124)
jungle 밀림, 정글(88)
just 방금, 오직(142)

## k

keep 계속하다(123)
key 열쇠(21)
kick 차다(123)
kill 죽이다, 없애다(123)
kind 친절한(136)
king 왕(40)
kitchen 부엌(21)
knee 무릎(12)
knife 칼(21)
knock 두드리다(124)
know 알다, 이해하다(124)

## l

lady 숙녀, 부인(55)
lake 호수(89)
land 땅, 육지(89)
large 큰(94)
last 마지막으로(143)
late 늦은, 늦게(136)
laugh 웃다(124)
lead 인도하다(40)
leaf 나뭇잎(89)
learn 배우다(46)
leave 떠나다(125)
left 왼쪽, 왼쪽의(98)
leg 다리(12)
lesson 수업(46)
let 시키다(124)
letter 편지(40)
library 도서관(47)
life 생명, 생활(40)
light⁽¹⁾ 가벼운(95)
light⁽²⁾ 빛, 조명(89)
like 좋아하다(109,125)
lion 사자(84)
lip 입술(13)
listen 듣다(65)
little 약간의(97,107,96)
live 살다(41)
lonely 외로운(137)
long 긴(108)
look 보다(125)
lot 많음(108)
loud 목소리가 큰(137)
love 사랑하다(125)
low 낮은(107)
luck 행운(113,41)
lunch 점심(74)

## m

ma'am  아주머니(25)
mad  미친, 열광한(137)
mail  우편(41)
make  만들다(125)
man  남자(55)
many  많은(96)
map  지도(79)
market  시장(49)
marry  결혼하다(41)
matter  문제, 곤란(65)
may  ~해도 좋다(126)
me  나를(4)
meat  고기(34)
meet  만나다(126)
men  man의 복수형(41)
mice  mouse의 복수형(84)
milk  우유(35)
million  100만(78)
mine  나의 것(9)
minute  분(78)
mirror  거울(22)
mom  엄마(26)
money  돈(50)
monkey  원숭이(84)
month  달(89)
moon  달(90)
morning  아침(74)
mother  어머니(26)
mountain  산(90)
mouth  입(13)
move  움직이다(126)
movie  영화(29)
much  많은(96)
music  음악(29)
must  꼭 해야만 한다(126)
my  나의(4)

## n

near  가까운(103)
neck  목(13)
new  새로운(137)
news  소식(42)
next  다음의, 다음에(137)
nice  멋진(138)
night  밤(74)

no  하나도 없는(138)
noon  정오, 한 낮(74)
north  북쪽(80)
nose  코(13)
not  아니다, 않다(143)
now  지금, 방금(143)
number  수, 숫자(78)
nurse  간호사(39)

## o

o'clock  ~시(정각)(78)
off  ~떨어져(143)
office  사무실(60)
old  늙은(99)
on  ~의 위에(99)
only  오직, 유일한(138)
open  열다(104)
orange  오렌지 색(52)
our  우리의(7)
ours  우리의 것(7)
out  밖으로, 밖에(103)

## p

page  페이지, 쪽(47)
paint  페인트(60)
pants  바지(15)
paper  종이(47)
parent  부모님(26)
party  파티, 모임(42)
pass  지나가다(126)
pay  지불하다(50)
peace  평화(42)
pear  (과일)배(37)
pen  펜(47)
pencil  연필(47)
people  사람들, 국민(55)
piano  피아노(29)
pick  따다(127)
picnic  소풍(61)
pig  돼지(85)
pilot  조종사(39)
pin  핀(48)
pink  분홍(52)
place  장소, 곳(61)
plant  식물(90)
play  연주하다, 놀다(127)

please  기쁘게 하다(127)
pocket  호주머니(15)
police  경찰(39)
pool  웅덩이, 연못(90)
poor  가난한(102,138)
pull  당기다(105)
push  밀다(104)
put  놓다, 두다(127)

## q

queen  여왕(42)
question  질문(65)
quick  빠른(96)
quiet  조용한(138)
quiz  질문, 퀴즈(66)

## r

radio  라디오(22)
rain  비, 비가오다(90)
rainbow  무지개(91)
ran  달렸다(127)
read  읽다, 낭독하다(66)
ready  준비가 된(139)
record  기록하다(128)
red  빨간색, 붉은(53)
remember  기억하다(128)
restaurant  레스토랑(61)
ribbon  리본(15)
rice  쌀, 밥(35)
rich  돈 많은(103)
ride  타다(128)
right  오른쪽(99)
ring  울리다(128)
ring  반지(16)
river  강(91)
road  길, 도로(61)
robot  로봇(53)
roof  지붕(22)
room  방(22)
round  둥근, 동그란(139)
run  달리다(128)

## s

sad  슬 픈(139,105)

safe  안전한(139)
salad  샐러드(35)
salt  소금(35)
same  동일한, 똑같은(139)
sand  모래(91)
school  학교, 수업(48)
sea  바다(91)
season  계절(74)
seat  자리, 좌석(61)
see  보다(129)
sell  팔다(96)
send  보내다(129)
set  한 벌, 짝, 세트(78)
shall  ~일 것이다(129)
she  그녀는, 그녀가(5)
sheep  양(85)
ship  배(57)
shoe  신, 구두(16)
shoot  쏘다, 던지다(129)
shop  가게(50)
short  짧은(109,99)
shout  소리치다(129)
show  보이다(130)
shut  닫다, 덮다(105)
silver  은, 은빛, 은의(91)
sing  노래, 노래하다(29)
sister  여자형제, 언니(26)
sit  앉다(104)
skate  스케이트(30)
skirt  스커트(16)
sky  하늘(92)
sled  썰매(57)
sleep  잠자다(42)
slide  미끄러지다(130)
slow  느린(113,97)
small  작은(95)
smell  냄새맡다(130)
smile  웃다, 미소지다(130)
snow  눈, 눈이오다(92)
so  정말로, 그렇게(143)
soap  비누(22)
soccer  축구(30)
sock  양말(17)
sofa  소파(23)
son  아들(26)
song  노래(30)
soon  곧(144)
sorry  죄송한(140)
south  남쪽(80)

150

space 공간, 우주(92)
speak 말하다(66)
spell 철자(66)
spend 낭비하다(130)
spoon 숟가락, 스푼(23)
sport 스포츠(30)
spring 봄(75)
stair 계단(23)
stamp 우표, 인지(43)
stand 서다, 일어서다(105)
star 별(92)
start 출발하다(102)
station 역, 정거장(62)
stop 멈추다(103)
store 가게, 상점(50)
story 이야기(67)
strawberry 딸기(37)
street 거리(62)
strike 때리다(131)
strong 힘이 센,강한(104)
student 학생(48)
study 공부하다(48)
stupid 어리석은(140)
subway 지하철(57)
sugar 설탕(35)
summer 여름(75)
sun 태양, 햇빛(92)
supermarket 슈퍼마켓(50)
supper 저녁식사(36)
sweater 스웨터(17)
swim 수영하다, 수영(30)
swing 그네(31)

**t**

table 테이블(48)
take 받다(112)
talk 말하다(67)
tall 키가 큰(98)

taste 맛을 보다(131)
taxi 택시(58)
teach 가르치다(49)
team 팀(31)
telephone 전화(23)
tell 말하다(67)
tennis 테니스(31)
test 시험, 검사(49)
thank 감사하다(140)
table 테이블(48)
take 받다(112)
talk 말하다(67)
tall 키가 큰(98)
taste 맛을 보다(131)
taxi 택시(58)
teach 가르치다(49)
team 팀(31)
telephone 전화(23)
tell 말하다(67)
tennis 테니스(31)
test 시험, 검사(49)
thank 감사하다(140)
that 저것, 그것(8)
the 그(9)
their 그들의(6)
them 그들을(7)
then 그 때, 그러면(144)
there 거기에(8)
these 이것들(8)
they 그들은(6)
thick 두꺼운(95)
thin 얇은(94,95)
think ~라고 생각하다(67)
this 이것(8)
those 그것들(8)
throw 던지다(131)
tie 넥타이(17)
tiger 호랑이(85)
time 시각, 시간(79)
today 오늘(75)

tomato 토마토(37)
tomorrow 내일(75)
tonight 오늘 밤(75)
tooth 이, 치아(13)
town 마을(43)
toy 장난감(53)
train 기차(58)
travel 여행, 여행하다(62)
tree 나무(93)
trip 여행(62)
truck 트럭(58)

**u**

umbrella 우산(17)
uncle 아저씨, 삼촌(27)
under ~의 아래에(98)
up 위쪽으로(99)
us 우리들을(7)

**v**

very 매우, 아주(144)
video 비디오(31)
village 마을, 촌락(43)
violin 바이올린(31)
visit 방문하다(80)

**w**

wait 기다리다(131)
walk 걷다, 산책하다(131)
warm 따뜻한(106)
was am,is의과거형(71)
water 물(93)
way 길, 방법(80)
we 우리, 저희가(7)

weak 약한(105)
week 주, 1주간(76)
welcome 환영하다(43)
well 만족하게, 잘(144)
were are의 과거형(71)
west 서쪽(80)
wet 젖은, 축축한(140)
what 무엇, 어떤(67)
when 언제(68)
where 어디에(68)
which 어느쪽, 어느(68)
white 흰, 흰빛(53)
who 누구(68)
whom 누구를(68)
whose 누구의(69)
why 왜(69)
wide 넓은(106)
wind 바람(93)
window 창(창문)(23)
winter 겨울(76)
wood 나무, 숲(93)
word 낱말, 단어(69)
world 세계, 지구(93)

**y**

year 년, 나이(79)
yellow 노랑(53)
yes 예, 네(69)
yesterday 어제(76)
you 너, 당신(4)
young 젊은, 어린(98)
your 너의, 너희들의(5)
yours 너의 것(9)

**z**

zero 0, 영(79)
zoo 동물원(85)

## 초등 영단어 750 따라쓰기

초판 5쇄 발행 2021년 5월 31일

글 Y&M 어학 연구소

**펴낸이** 서영희 | **펴낸곳** 와이 앤 엠

**편집** 임명아 | **책임교정** 하연정

**본문인쇄** 명성 인쇄 | **제책** 정화 제책

**제작** 이윤식 | **마케팅** 강성태

주소 120-848 서울시 서대문구 홍은동 376-28

전화 (02)308-3891 | Fax (02)308-3892

E-mail yam3891@naver.com

등록 2007년 8월 29일 제312-2007-000040호

ISBN 978-89-93557-32-9  63740

본사는 출판물 윤리강령을 준수합니다.